HOW TO TALK TO ANYONE: A GUIDE FOR YOUNG PROFESSIONALS

MASTERING COMMUNICATION SKILLS TO BUILD CONNECTIONS AND CONFIDENCE

ELLIOTT MIDDLETON PHD

To effectively communicate, we must realize that we are all different in the way we perceive the world and use this understanding as a guide to our communication with others.

— TONY ROBBINS

INTRODUCTION

Have you ever found yourself at a gathering, clutching a drink, scanning the room, and feeling your stomach knot as you tried to muster the courage to join a conversation? Many of us know this scenario all too well: the palpable discomfort, the silent self-coaching, and the overwhelming desire to connect, blocked by invisible barriers of anxiety and uncertainty. This universal struggle to communicate, reach out, and genuinely connect is not just a social challenge but a pivotal aspect of our human experience.

I'm Elliott Middleton, PhD. Once a college professor and decision scientist, I spent years immersed in university research and global business, analyzing data to predict risk and make decisions. However, the human element—the subtle nuances of communication that influenced those decisions—captivated me and steered my career in a new direction. My transition from data to dialogue, from numbers to narratives, began a journey into understanding the art and science of communication. This book is a culmination of that journey; it reviews the best literature I could find on interpersonal communication, especially in business and the professions. I can't claim that the recommendations you'll find within are all original, but I can say that

I vetted every one of them against my experience. Honestly, I wish I'd had this book when I was starting out.

The mission of *How to Talk to Anyone: Proven Strategies for Introverts, Extroverts, and Everyone In-Between* is simple yet ambitious: to arm you with actionable, practical strategies to enhance your communicative prowess. Whether you're an introvert who struggles to share your thoughts, an extrovert who wants to refine your approach, or someone who wants to improve at making meaningful connections, this book is for you. Here, you'll learn to communicate and do so with confidence and authenticity, deepening your relationships in every sphere of your life.

In today's fast-paced world, where digital communications often replace face-to-face interactions, conversing effectively is more crucial than ever. Strong communication skills can improve personal relationships, enhance careers, and significantly boost overall life satisfaction. Yet, despite their importance, many find it challenging to navigate the complexities of human interaction.

This book is structured to guide you through practical, engaging chapters that blend psychological insights with real-world scenarios and hands-on exercises. Each chapter is designed to build on the knowledge gained from the previous one, forming a ladder of skills that will elevate your communicative abilities. From initiating conversations with strangers to deepening long-standing relationships, the strategies you'll learn are intended for immediate application, ensuring you can see the benefits from the first page.

Through personal anecdotes from my own experiences—be it in professional settings, cross-cultural negotiations, or everyday interactions—I'll share the lessons that have reshaped my approach to communication. These stories will highlight challenges, connections, and breakthroughs that effective communication can foster.

As you embark on this journey, I encourage you to keep an open mind and actively experiment with the strategies discussed. Communication is a skill that can be honed through practice and persistence. Your effort will directly impact the richness of your interactions and the breadth of your social and professional networks.

Let's start this journey with the promise that the skills you develop here will enhance your conversations, transform your relationships, and broaden your world. The ability to talk to anyone is not an innate gift but a set of skills that can be learned, practiced, and perfected. Are you ready to take the first step?

Here's to more fulfilling conversations, stronger connections, and a more confident you. Let's begin.

1

MASTERING THE ART OF FIRST IMPRESSIONS

First impressions are both fleeting moments and long-lasting imprints, a paradox that can define the trajectory of personal and professional relationships. Have you ever considered the weight of a first meeting or the lasting impact of an initial conversation? Whether it's a job interview, a networking event, or a casual social gathering, how you introduce yourself can set the stage for the following relationship. This chapter is dedicated to turning those crucial first seconds into a powerful tool for connection and opportunity.

1.1 Crafting Your Introduction: The Elevator Pitch

In networking and professional growth, the "elevator pitch" is a fundamental tool many struggle to perfect. An elevator pitch is a brief, persuasive speech that sparks interest in your work. It should be concise enough to deliver during a short elevator ride—hence the name. An elevator pitch's core purpose is to inform, engage, and intrigue your listener, providing a snapshot of who you are, what you do, and why it matters.

Structure and Content

Crafting an effective elevator pitch requires a clear understanding of its components. Start with who you are—this isn't just your job title but a brief insight into your professional identity and personal ethos. Follow this with what you do; here, specificity is critical. Rather than saying, "I work in marketing," you could say, "I create targeted social media campaigns for independent bookstores to increase their online presence and sales." Finally, address why it matters—this is where you connect your professional actions to a broader impact, which helps your listener understand the value of what you do.

The structure of your pitch should be simple but impactful, distilled into no more than 30 seconds of speaking. This brevity forces you to carefully consider the most essential elements of your message, ensuring clarity and immediacy in your delivery.

Tailoring the Pitch

A common mistake is to have a one-size-fits-all approach to your elevator pitch. The most effective pitches are those adapted to the listener and the situation. Consider the interests and background of your audience—are they industry peers, potential employers, or maybe a casual acquaintance interested in your field? This understanding can shape the emphasis of your pitch, tailoring it to resonate with the listener's needs and interests. For instance, if speaking to a potential employer, focus on your achievements and how they align with the company's goals. Conversely, at a social event, your pitch might be less about impressing and more about making a personal connection, highlighting shared interests or experiences.

Practice Techniques

Practicing your elevator pitch is as crucial as creating it. One effective method is to practice in front of a mirror or record yourself. This allows you to see and hear how you come across, making refining your tone, pacing, and body language easier. Additionally, consider practicing with friends or mentors who can provide constructive feedback and suggest adjustments.

Another helpful technique is the mirroring exercise. This involves practicing your pitch with a partner who mirrors your physical gestures and vocal tone. This exercise can be illuminating, as it helps you gauge the naturalness and authenticity of your delivery, encouraging adjustments to ensure your pitch feels genuine and engaging.

Interactive Element: Elevator Pitch Worksheet

To aid in developing your elevator pitch, I've included an activity that breaks down the pitch into its key components:

- **Who You Are:** Write a sentence about your professional identity and personal ethos.
- **What You Do:** Describe your current role or project with as much specificity as possible.
- **Why It Matters:** Explain the impact or value of your work in a broader context.

Use this exercise to draft, refine, and tailor your elevator pitch for different audiences and situations. This will ensure you're always prepared to present effectively, no matter the context.

1.2 The Psychology Behind First Impressions: What Sticks

Many rapid assessments occur within a few seconds when you meet someone for the first time. These assessments, often unconscious, significantly influence your initial perception of the person. A cornerstone of these assessments is the role of cognitive biases such as the halo and primacy effects. The halo effect occurs when an initial positive impression makes us make favorable assumptions about a person in other areas. For example, if someone is dressed impeccably, you might instantly assume they are successful or competent. Conversely, the primacy effect highlights our tendency to prioritize the first information we encounter about a person. For instance, the first few words spoken in an introduction can disproportionately shape our overall impression of that individual.

Understanding these biases is crucial for anyone keen on making a positive impression. Awareness allows us to strategically present ourselves in ways that align with how human cognition typically operates. For example, knowing that people tend to remember the first thing you say, it becomes pivotal to craft the opening line of your introduction carefully. Similarly, presenting a visually tidy and appealing appearance can capitalize on the halo effect, subtly influencing others' perceptions toward a more favorable view without realizing it.

The emotional responses elicited during these first encounters are equally powerful. Emotions play a significant role in how memories are formed. Positive emotions, in particular, can make an experience or interaction more memorable. Therefore, inducing a positive emotional response in someone can make your interaction more memorable. This can be achieved through various means, from the enthusiasm and warmth in your voice to genuine compliments or engaging stories that evoke laughter or joy. Every emotional exchange during a first meeting acts like a brushstroke in the overall picture that someone will remember about you.

Consistency in your verbal and non-verbal cues also plays a fundamental role in first impressions. When your words match your body language, you project authenticity and trustworthiness. For example, claiming to be thrilled about meeting someone while maintaining a flat tone and closed body posture sends mixed signals that confuse the listener and may lead them to question your sincerity. On the other hand, when your expressions, gestures, and words are aligned, it strengthens the believability of your message, thereby enhancing your overall impression.

To leverage these psychological insights effectively, one must employ strategic communication tactics right from the start of an interaction. One such strategy is using open-ended questions, which serve multiple purposes. First, it signals your interest in the other person, making them feel valued and more likely to view you positively. Second, it invites them to share more about themselves, providing deeper insights into their interests and personality, which you can use to tailor your interaction further to engage them effectively. For instance, asking, "What inspired you to start your career in architecture?" can elicit a more detailed and personal response than a simple "What do you do?" This makes the conversation more engaging and increases the likelihood that they will remember you as someone who made them feel excited and heard.

Incorporating these psychological strategies into your approach to first encounters can transform simple introductions into memorable connections. By understanding and adapting to the inherent biases in human perception, managing the emotional tone of your interactions, ensuring consistency in your communication, and engaging others with thoughtful questions, you set the stage for positive, lasting impressions that could pave the way for meaningful relationships, both personally and professionally.

1.3 The Role of Body Language in Greeting Others

Body language, often considered the unspoken element of communication, plays a pivotal role in our impressions and how others perceive us. When you meet someone, your body language begins to speak for you before a single word is exchanged. It is a powerful tool that, when used effectively, can open doors to meaningful connections. The fundamentals of positive body language in greetings involve a confident posture, purposeful gestures, and direct eye contact. A confident posture, standing tall with shoulders back and head held high, conveys self-assurance and openness. It makes you appear approachable and ready to engage. Purposeful gestures, such as a nod or a slight lean towards the person you are interacting with, can express interest and attentiveness. Meanwhile, maintaining eye contact shows confidence and respect for the person you speak to, signaling that you are fully present.

Cultural sensitivity is crucial when considering body language, as positive gestures in one culture may be perceived differently in another. For instance, while direct eye contact is valued in many Western cultures as a sign of honesty and confidence, in some Asian cultures, it might be seen as aggressive or disrespectful. Similarly, the physical distance maintained during a conversation can vary significantly across cultures. In many Latin American cultures, closer physical proximity during a conversation can indicate warmth and friendliness, whereas in Nordic cultures, more personal space is often preferred. Understanding these cultural nuances is essential to communicating effectively and respectfully in our increasingly globalized world. It prevents misinterpretations and helps build rapport with people from diverse backgrounds.

The handshake, a familiar gesture in many cultures, is often the cornerstone of first meetings. A good handshake's nuances can significantly influence an interaction's dynamics. A strong, firm handshake conveys confidence and establishes a connection. It should be accompanied by appropriate eye contact and a slight smile to enhance the warmth of the greeting. However, adapting the handshake according to the cultural context and personal comfort is essential. In some cultures, a softer handshake is the norm, or alternative greetings such as a nod or a bow may be more appropriate. Being adaptable and observant can help you navigate these situations smoothly and ensure that your greeting respects cultural norms and personal boundaries.

To apply these body language concepts practically, consider engaging in role-play scenarios that mimic real-life interactions. This can be particularly useful in a workshop or training environment, where participants can practice greetings and introductions with peer feedback. For instance, role-playing in a job interview setting can help individuals practice maintaining a confident posture, using purposeful gestures, and delivering a firm handshake, all while receiving constructive feedback. Such exercises enhance understanding of effective body language and build confidence in using these skills in everyday interactions.

Incorporating these aspects of body language into your greeting rituals can transform your approach to new interactions. By being mindful of your posture, gestures, eye contact, and cultural nuances and practicing these elements in various settings, you can significantly improve how you connect with others. Whether in a professional networking event, a social gathering, or a multicultural setting, mastering the subtleties of body language can lead to more positive and impactful first impressions.

1.4 Dressing for Success: Aligning Appearance with Intent

The way we dress speaks volumes before we even utter a word. Our clothing and grooming are not merely about aesthetic appeal but also critical components of our non-verbal communication, shaping others' perceptions and expectations. In professional settings, the importance of dressing appropriately must be considered. Each industry has its own set of norms and expectations regarding attire, and navigating these can significantly impact your professional image and, by extension, your career advancement. For instance, attire in a creative industry like graphic design may differ vastly from that in a corporate legal office. Personal expression through clothing might be encouraged in creative fields, reflecting innovative thinking and originality. Conversely, conventional business attire in more traditional corporate environments can signify professionalism and respect for organizational norms and expectations.

However, the challenge often lies in balancing personal style with professional expectations. It's about finding a way to express individuality without compromising the perceived professionalism that specific industries demand. This balance can be particularly crucial during job interviews, where first impressions are pivotal. For example, wearing a tailored suit to an interview for a banking position shows conformity to industry standards. Yet, the choice of tie or accessories could reflect a touch of personal style. It's about making strategic clothing choices that align with professional norms while allowing room for individual expression that stands out correctly.

Visual harmony in attire involves more than just dressing for the occasion; it's about choosing colors and styles that enhance your features and convey the desired message. Colors can have a pronounced psychological impact—blue, for example, often denotes stability and trustworthiness and can be a good choice for interviews or important meetings. Similarly, the fit and style of clothing should complement your body shape, ensuring that clothes are neither too tight nor too loose. This attention to detail improves how others perceive you and boosts your confidence, which is crucial when making an impression.

Moreover, grooming and maintenance play an indispensable role in your professional presentation. Regular grooming habits, such as ensuring well-styled hair, trimmed nails, and neat attire, are fundamental. These elements of personal care are often taken as indicators of how individuals manage responsibilities—sloppiness in attire can be misconstrued as a lax attitude towards work. For those in client-facing roles or positions of authority, the stakes are even higher, as your appearance can influence people's trust and respect towards you.

Consider, for instance, a consultant meeting a new client for a contract discussion. The consultant's polished appearance, from a well-fitted suit and groomed hair to clean, polished shoes, can immediately convey a sense of professionalism and attention to detail, setting the tone for the meeting. This doesn't mean overspending on high-end brands; instead, it's about mindful selection of clothing and regular maintenance to ensure a neat, professional appearance at all times.

In practical terms, maintaining a wardrobe that fits well and is appropriate for various professional settings can involve regular reviews and updates of your attire, ensuring that clothes are in good repair and continue to fit well. Seasonal adjustments are also significant, not only for comfort but also to match the environmental context of your meetings or workplace. Additionally, investing in quality over quantity—choosing well-made pieces that will last longer and look better—can make maintaining a professional wardrobe more straightforward and cost-effective.

Navigating these aspects of professional dress does not require conformity at the expense of personality. Instead, it's about making informed choices that align your style with professional standards, enhancing how you are perceived and, ultimately, how you perceive yourself. These choices are not just about making a good impression but about feeling confident and prepared for the opportunities and challenges of the professional world.

1.5 The Power of a Smile: Authenticity in Action

The simple act of smiling carries more weight in communication than most of us realize. It's not just a universal sign of happiness but a powerful tool that can set the tone for interactions, influence mood, and open up channels of communication that might otherwise remain closed. Smiling genuinely does more than signal friendliness; it creates an environment where open, honest communication can flourish. Psychological studies have consistently shown that people see you as more likable, courteous, and competent when you smile. This is particularly intriguing in professional environments where first impressions can dictate the future of business relationships.

One of the most compelling aspects of smiling is its ability to enhance perceived trustworthiness. Research published in the *Journal of Experimental Social Psychology* suggests that when individuals smile genuinely, they are often perceived as more trustworthy than those who do not. This perception stems from the evolutionary cues associated with smiling—signals of non-threat and friendliness that are hardwired into our brains. Furthermore, a smile can influence the mood of both the giver and the receiver; it's a natural way to release endorphins, improving your mood and the atmosphere of the interaction. This biochemical shift makes you feel better and enhances your ability to connect with others, making interactions more productive and enjoyable.

However, smiling in professional contexts must be balanced with authenticity. Over-smiling or forcing a smile in inappropriate situations can backfire, making you appear insincere or manipulative. The key is to employ a smile that aligns with the situation and feels natural. For instance, a gentle, confident smile can be effective during a business negotiation, conveying ease and assurance. It suggests you are approachable, open to dialogue, and confident in your position and discussion.

Practicing genuine smiling is an art that can be honed with simple exercises. One effective practice is to recall a genuinely happy or amusing moment before entering a professional setting where you anticipate the need for impactful communication. This mental recall can help elicit a genuine smile that will naturally carry the positive emotions of the memory into your interaction. Another exercise is practicing smiling in front of a mirror to identify what a natural smile feels like. Please pay attention to the eyes as a genuine smile reaches them, causing them to crinkle slightly. This is often called the 'Duchenne smile,' named after the researcher who first distinguished the muscle movements involved in genuine versus forced smiles.

Regularly incorporating these practices can significantly enhance your ability to deploy a smile effectively and authentically in both personal and professional contexts. By doing so, you not only improve how others perceive you but also create a more favorable environment for yourself and those you interact with. Remember, a smile is not just a courtesy; it's a powerful tool for opening doors to deeper, more meaningful connections.

2

EFFECTIVE COMMUNICATION TECHNIQUES

Imagine you're at a bustling coffee shop, engrossed in a conversation. The aroma of freshly brewed coffee wafts through the air, mingling with the hum of background chatter. Here, amidst the clatter of cups and the occasional hiss of the espresso machine, lies a golden opportunity to transform how you connect with others. This chapter focuses on a foundational skill often overlooked yet paramount to fostering meaningful relationships: active listening.

2.1 Active Listening: More Than Just Hearing

Active listening is an intentional act of absorbing the information presented by others, not just audibly, but with full engagement of mind and spirit. Unlike passive hearing, which is the involuntary act of perceiving sound, active listening involves focusing on and understanding the speaker's message. It's about immersing yourself in the conversation, processing what's being said, and responding thoughtfully. The power of active listening lies in its ability to enhance interpersonal relations, build trust, and ensure mutual understanding—critical ingredients for effective communication.

Key Techniques

The art of active listening is anchored in several techniques that signal attentiveness and respect to your conversation partner. **Paraphrasing** involves restating what the speaker has said in your own words—a way to confirm that you have understood their message correctly and to show that you are engaged. **Summarizing**, on the other hand, involves condensing the speaker's main points and expressing them succinctly, which not only keeps the conversation focused but also helps clarify the discussion's purpose. **Reflecting feelings**, another crucial technique, requires you to identify and articulate the emotions underlying the speaker's words. This empathetic response acknowledges the speaker's feelings, validating their experience and deepening your connection.

Barriers to Effective Listening

Despite its apparent simplicity, active listening is often hindered by several barriers. Distractions are a primary obstacle—whether environmental, like the noise in a coffee shop, or internal, such as wandering thoughts or preconceived notions about the topic or speaker. Preconceptions can lead you to filter or alter what you hear, thus undermining the listening process. Emotional reactions can also impede active listening; strong feelings might trigger defensive responses or cause you to jump to conclusions before the speaker has finished.

To overcome these barriers, it's essential to cultivate an environment conducive to effective listening. This might mean choosing a quiet setting or consciously clearing your mind of distractions before engaging in a conversation. It also involves monitoring and controlling emotional reactions by remaining neutral and open, regardless of the discussion's content.

Listening Exercises

One way to enhance your active listening skills is through **focused listening sessions**. These exercises involve listening to a speech or a conversation and recounting the message with as much detail and accuracy as possible. This practice improves your concentration and helps you better retain and process information.

Another effective exercise is **listening with the intent to learn** rather than respond. In this exercise, approach conversations with curiosity and the primary goal of learning something new from the speaker. This shift in perspective can dramatically change how you engage in conversations, making them more informative and enriching for both parties involved.

Interactive Element: Reflective Journaling Prompt

Consider starting a listening journal. After each significant conversation, take a moment to jot down key points you gathered, how well you think you understood the speaker, and what emotions and thoughts you experienced during the interaction. Reflect on how effectively you managed distractions and your emotional reactions. This self-reflection will provide insights into your listening habits and help you identify areas for improvement, enhancing your overall communicative competence.

By mastering active listening, you become a better communicator and a more empathetic and connected individual. The skills developed through active listening extend beyond personal conversations and are equally effective in professional settings, enriching your interactions and broadening your understanding of the world. As you practice and refine these techniques, you'll find that genuinely listening can transform the quality of your relationships and deepen your engagement with others, one conversation at a time.

2.2 Asking the Right Questions to Deepen Conversations

In any conversation, the questions you ask are more than just a pathway to information; they are a bridge to deeper understanding and connection. The art of questioning, when mastered, can transform superficial interactions into rich, engaging dialogues that leave both parties feeling understood and valued. To navigate this art, you must understand the types of questions you can employ: closed and open-ended. Each serves a unique purpose in communication. Closed questions typically elicit a yes or no answer and help gather specific information quickly and decisively. They help clarify details and confirm facts, making them indispensable in conversations where precision is critical. However, their scope is limited when exploring thoughts and feelings. This is where open-ended questions come into play. These questions, framed to encourage a detailed response, open the floor for discussion, allowing the speaker to express thoughts, feelings, and opinions. They invite elaboration, which can lead to richer, more informative exchanges. For instance, instead of asking, "Did you enjoy the event?" which limits the answer to a simple yes or no, asking, "What did you enjoy about the event?" encourages sharing specific experiences and insights, deepening the conversation.

Strategic questioning takes this further by using questions to steer the conversation in meaningful directions. It's about asking the right question at the right time to achieve a specific outcome, whether building rapport, solving a problem, or gaining a deeper understanding of the person you're speaking with. This strategy involves thoughtful questions tailored to the interaction's context and purpose. For example, in a professional setting, strategic questioning can help you uncover what motivates your colleagues, thereby fostering a collaborative work environment. It's about being purposeful with your inquiries, which requires active listening and understanding the conversation's flow. This deliberate approach not only garners more comprehensive responses but also signals to your conversation partner that you are genuinely interested in their perspective, enhancing the overall quality of the interaction.

Empathetic questioning is another layer in the art of inquiry that focuses on building emotional connections. These questions are designed to demonstrate empathy and understanding, showing that you hear and feel the impact of what is being shared. Empathetic questioning requires a sensitive approach to how questions are framed and delivered. It involves recognizing the emotional content of the conversation and responding in a way that validates the speaker's feelings. For example, if someone discusses a challenging personal experience, an empathetic question might be, "That sounds challenging. How did that situation make you feel?" This not only acknowledges the difficulty of the situation but also invites the speaker to share more about their emotional journey. Such questions can deepen mutual understanding and trust, fostering a closer connection between the participants in the conversation.

To put these concepts into practice, role-playing scenarios can be incredibly effective. These scenarios allow you to experiment with questions in a controlled, reflective environment. Imagine a scenario where you are trying to understand a friend's decision to change careers. Through role-playing, you could practice framing open-ended questions like, "What inspired you to take this new direction?" and empathetic questions like, "How are you feeling about this big change?" Each role-playing session offers a safe space to refine your questioning techniques, adjust your approach based on the responses you receive, and receive feedback. This hands-on practice is invaluable in honing your ability to ask thoughtful, impactful questions that can transform everyday conversations into meaningful exchanges. By integrating these questioning techniques into your communication toolkit, you equip yourself to navigate various social interactions more effectively, making every conversation an opportunity for deeper connection and understanding.

2.3 Reading Nonverbal Cues: A Guide to Body Language

The subtle sway of a conversation doesn't rely solely on spoken words; nonverbal cues such as facial expressions, gestures, and posture hold immense power in shaping interpersonal interactions. Imagine walking into a room and seeing someone with crossed arms and a furrowed brow. Without a single word, you might interpret these signals as resistance or discomfort, prompting a cautious approach. This is the essence of nonverbal communication—it speaks volumes in silence and is vital in decoding the unspoken elements of dialogue.

Facial expressions are the most immediate indicators of a person's emotions and intentions. A smile can indicate openness and friendliness, while a scowl might suggest displeasure or disagreement. However, the interpretation of these expressions can vary widely. For instance, a smile in one cultural context might be a genuine expression of pleasure, while in another, it could be a polite mask for discomfort or even disapproval. Beyond facial expressions, nodding signifies agreement or encouragement to continue speaking. At the same time, a hand raised with the palm outward can signal a desire to pause or interrupt. When read correctly, these gestures can guide the flow of conversation and enhance understanding.

Posture also plays a crucial role in communication. An upright posture can convey confidence and attentiveness, making the speaker appear more credible and engaging. In contrast, a slumped posture might be read as a lack of interest or low energy, potentially disengaging the audience. However, the context again significantly influences interpretation. For example, in a casual setting among close friends, a relaxed posture might communicate ease and comfort, fostering a more open and intimate exchange.

Interpreting these nonverbal signals accurately requires keen observation and understanding of their potential ambiguities. Misinterpretations can lead to misunderstandings that may distort the intended message of the interaction. For instance, rapid blinking might be perceived as a sign of nervousness or deceit. However, if someone just adjusted their contact lenses, this action might be a physiological response rather than a cue of emotional distress or dishonesty. Recognizing such nuances is vital to avoiding false judgments and fostering more transparent communication.

Cultural variations in nonverbal communication add another layer of complexity. Gestures considered polite and cheerful in one culture may be offensive in another. For example, the thumbs-up gesture is commonly used in the United States to denote approval or agreement; however, it can be considered rude or offensive in parts of the Middle East. Similarly, the concept of personal space varies between cultures. In some cultures, close proximity during a conversation might signify trust and friendship; in others, it could be seen as intrusive or disrespectful. Thus, cultural sensitivity is crucial when interpreting body language across different cultural contexts. It requires an awareness of these differences and an openness to learning from each interaction to avoid cultural faux pas and build more meaningful and respectful relationships.

To improve your ability to read and respond to nonverbal cues, consider engaging in people-watching exercises in public spaces where you can observe various interactions. For example, spend an hour in a busy public area like a park or a shopping mall and watch the interactions around you without being able to hear them. Focus on interpreting people's facial expressions, gestures, and postures without the influence of spoken words. Try to infer the nature of their interactions: Are they friendly, tense, or formal? What nonverbal signals led you to these conclusions? This exercise enhances your observational skills and helps you appreciate the subtleties of body language in different contexts.

By developing a sharper awareness and a deeper understanding of nonverbal communication, you equip yourself with the tools to navigate complex social landscapes more effectively. Whether in personal relationships, professional settings, or cross-cultural interactions, interpreting body language enhances your communication skills, fostering stronger connections and minimizing the potential for misunderstanding. As you continue to observe and interact, remember that each gesture, each expression, and each posture is a piece of the larger conversation, offering insights that words alone cannot provide.

2.4 The Art of Mirroring: Building Rapport Quickly

Mirroring subtly replicates another person's body language, speech patterns, or attitudes. Rooted deeply in the psychological mechanisms of empathy and social bonding, mirroring can be a powerful tool to build rapport and establish trust quickly. When you mirror someone during a conversation, you subconsciously signal that you are in sync with them, making the interaction smoother and more engaging. This phenomenon is a conscious strategy and a natural process often occurring among closely connected people such as friends or family members.

Understanding how to mirror effectively involves more than merely copying gestures or mimics; it's about attuning to the other person's emotions and energy. Adequate mirroring should be subtle and natural rather than overt and mimetic. For instance, if your conversation partner leans forward slightly while speaking, you might do the same to indicate engagement rather than replicating every move they make, which can seem contrived. The key is in the details—adjusting your speech rate to match theirs, adopting a similar tone, or using shared phrases can all contribute to a sense of harmony and comfort between you and the person you are communicating with.

Mirroring can prove beneficial in a variety of contexts. In negotiations, for example, mirroring the other person's body language can create a non-verbal agreement, easing tensions and fostering a cooperative atmosphere. In sales, mirroring a client's posture and speech patterns can help establish a connection, making the client feel understood and valued, leading to better transactional outcomes. Even in casual conversations, mirroring can enhance the social bond and make the interaction more enjoyable and fluid. It signals that you are paying attention and genuinely interested in the interaction, qualities most people appreciate sincerely in any social setting.

Practicing adequate mirroring can be developed through simple exercises. One practical method is to engage in casual conversations with friends or colleagues and consciously adopt one or two nonverbal cues that they use. This could involve using similar hand gestures or mirroring their sitting posture. The aim is not to mimic but to subtly reflect their communication style. Over time, this practice can help you become more attuned to others' nonverbal signals and use mirroring more instinctively.

Another exercise involves watching interviews on television or online. Observe how the interviewer and the guest interact, paying close attention to body language, tone of voice, and speaking tempo. Try to discern instances where mirroring occurs and note how it influences the flow of the conversation. This observational exercise can provide insights into how mirroring facilitates smoother communication and help you apply these observations in your interactions.

By integrating mirroring into your communication repertoire, you subtly enhance your interactions, making them more engaging and effective. Whether you want to build rapport quickly in a professional setting or connect better with friends and family, understanding and practicing the art of mirroring can significantly enrich your communication skills and deepen your relationships.

2.5 Tailoring Your Message According to the Audience

Understanding your audience is the cornerstone of effective communication. It's like being a chef; just as a chef adjusts recipes to cater to various dietary preferences and palates, a skilled communicator modifies their message to resonate with different audiences. To tailor your message effectively, you must thoroughly analyze your audience's demographics, cultural backgrounds, interests, and potential biases. This involves gathering data on age, gender, profession, cultural sensitivities, and even political orientations where relevant. Such analysis can often reveal the audience's expectations, which helps craft messages that reach and impact them.

For instance, when addressing a group of young tech enthusiasts at a conference, your message might focus on the latest technological trends and jargon they are familiar with. In contrast, a presentation to senior executives might require a more formal tone and focus on ROI and risk management. Each scenario demands a different approach regarding content, language, and delivery style. Adapting your message based on a clear understanding of your audience is crucial to ensure clarity and comprehension and build trust and credibility.

Once the message is crafted and delivered, the next crucial step is incorporating feedback. This involves an active listening loop where verbal and non-verbal responses refine and adjust your communication. Feedback can come during or after your interaction and take various forms, from direct comments to engagement metrics on digital platforms. For example, if you notice dwindling attention or puzzled looks during a workshop, you might need to simplify your language or provide more examples to clarify complex points. In digital communications, analytics tools can show you which parts of your message engage the audience and which are not, allowing for real-time adjustments.

Let's consider a case study from a marketing campaign for a multinational beverage company. The campaign was initially launched with the same messaging across multiple countries. However, feedback showed that while the campaign was successful in Europe, it resonated less in East Asian markets. Further analysis revealed cultural differences in beverage consumption behaviors and perceptions. The company then adjusted its messages to align with each region's cultural values and preferences, significantly improving engagement and sales. This example underscores the importance of flexibility and responsiveness in communication strategies, demonstrating how tailored content, grounded in audience understanding and responsive to feedback, can lead to better outcomes.

By continuously analyzing your audience, adapting your messages, and integrating feedback, you develop a dynamic communication strategy that addresses the audience's current needs and anticipates future changes. This approach ensures sustained engagement and leaves a lasting impact, making your communications heard, felt, and remembered.

As we wrap up this chapter on effective communication techniques, remember that the essence of good communication lies in what you say and how and to whom you are saying it. Each interaction is an opportunity to learn more about your audience, refine your message, and enhance your delivery. With the skills and strategies outlined here—from active listening and strategic questioning to understanding nonverbal cues and mirroring—you are better equipped to navigate the nuances of effective communication in diverse settings. Looking ahead, the next chapter will delve into overcoming communication barriers, where we'll explore strategies to deal with common obstacles that hinder effective exchange, ensuring that your message not only reaches but truly connects with the audience.

3

OVERCOMING COMMUNICATION
BARRIERS

Navigating the complexities of social interactions can sometimes feel like trying to speak a foreign language, especially for those who identify as introverts. It's a quiet evening, and you're at a lively party, surrounded by chatter and laughter. While others seem to mingle effortlessly, you find yourself clinging to the outskirts, rehearsing lines in your head, and waiting for the right moment to join in. This scenario is not just expected but a significant hurdle for many. This chapter explores methods for overcoming such communication barriers, focusing first on strategies explicitly tailored for introverts. Understanding and embracing your introverted qualities, managing your energy wisely, and gradually building your social confidence can transform your communication experiences from draining to enriching.

3.1 Strategies for Introverts: Thriving in Social Settings

Understanding Introversion

Introversion is a personality trait characterized by a preference for quieter, more reflective environments instead of seeking out high-stimulation social settings. Far from being a flaw, introversion is simply a different way of engaging with the world. Introverts often find deep satisfaction in solitary activities or discussions on topics of interest and may feel drained after prolonged social interactions. This doesn't mean introverts are poor communicators; they have a different communication style. They are typically reflective, thoughtful conversationalists who offer significant depth and insight when they do choose to speak. Understanding this trait allows introverts to leverage their strengths—such as keen observation and deep thinking—into effective communication strategies.

Energy Management

For introverts, managing social energy is crucial. Recognizing when to take breaks during social interactions can prevent feelings of exhaustion. It's important to acknowledge that stepping away to recharge is okay by finding a quiet corner during a party or excusing yourself for a few minutes of solitude. Effective energy management also involves planning social activities to ensure they are followed by rest periods. Arranging your social calendar this way can help you engage more fully when participating, making social interactions less daunting and more enjoyable.

Selective Participation

Choosing social settings that align with your interests can significantly improve your experience. Instead of forcing yourself into large, noisy gatherings, seek out smaller, more intimate settings where in-depth conversations about topics you are passionate about are more likely to occur. Engaging in activities and discussions you are genuinely interested in makes interactions more enjoyable and increases your likelihood of connecting with like-minded individuals, making socializing feel more natural and less draining.

Building Confidence in Small Steps

For many introverts, initiating a conversation can be intimidating. Start small by setting achievable goals for yourself, such as initiating a brief discussion with a colleague or asking a question during a meeting. These small steps can significantly boost your confidence over time. Practicing your conversational skills in less intimidating settings, such as with close friends or family, can also prepare you for more challenging social situations. Over time, these practices build a foundation of confidence that makes more significant or formal social interactions more manageable.

Interactive Element: Reflective Journaling Prompt

Keep a journal dedicated to your social interactions to develop your social strategies further. After each social event, write down what went well, what challenges you faced, and how you felt before, during, and after the interactions. Reflect on the energy management techniques you used and how effective they were. This reflective practice can provide valuable insights into your communication style and help you develop more effective strategies tailored to your introverted nature.

By embracing and understanding your introversion, strategically managing your energy, selecting appropriate social settings, and building confidence through gradual exposure, you can transform your approach to communication. These strategies allow you to engage on your terms, turning potential barriers into opportunities for meaningful interaction. Whether at a casual meet-up or a professional networking event, you can navigate social spaces with greater ease and confidence, making the most of your unique qualities as an introvert.

3.2 Handling Social Anxiety: Practical Tips and Exercises

Social anxiety can turn everyday interactions into daunting challenges. Picture yourself entering a crowded room or preparing to speak up in a meeting. For many, these situations trigger a rush of nervousness that isn't just unpleasant but also quite limiting. Understanding what triggers your social anxiety is the first step toward managing it effectively. It involves paying close attention to the scenarios that heighten your anxiety and noting your physical and emotional responses. For some, large groups might be the trigger, while formal settings or speaking on the spot can cause discomfort for others. By pinpointing these triggers, you can understand the underlying fears—

perhaps a fear of judgment, making mistakes, or feeling out of place.

Once you've identified your triggers, cognitive behavioral techniques can transform how you perceive and react to these anxieties. These strategies involve recognizing and challenging the negative thoughts that arise during anxious moments. For instance, if you're worried about stumbling over your words during a speech, you might automatically think, "I'm going to embarrass myself, and everyone will think less of me." Cognitive restructuring allows you to challenge this thought by asking, "Do I have evidence to support this thought, or am I assuming the worst?" More often than not, you'll find that your fears are not entirely grounded in reality. By continually practicing this technique, you can gradually shift your mindset to one that is more balanced and less dominated by fear, reducing the intensity of your anxiety over time.

Physical strategies such as relaxation and grounding exercises can be powerful tools alongside cognitive techniques. Deep breathing is more than a cliché; it's a physiologically proven method to calm the nervous system. Focusing on slow, deep breaths can decrease your heart rate and immediately lower stress levels. Mindfulness and grounding techniques also play a crucial role. These might involve focusing on sensory experiences—what you can see, hear, touch, taste, and smell—to anchor you in the present moment and draw your attention away from overwhelming thoughts. This practice not only helps in managing acute anxiety but also enhances your overall sense of mental presence, making you more resilient in the face of stress.

One of the most effective yet challenging strategies is guided exposure. This technique involves gradual exposure to the social situations you fear in a controlled and systematic way. Starting small might mean practicing speaking up in smaller, more familiar groups before tackling more significant, more intimidating gatherings. Each exposure should be planned and deliberate, with a clear objective. For example, you might aim to ask at least one question during a meeting or initiate a brief conversation with a stranger at a social event. After each exposure, reflect on the experience, focusing on what went well and what you can improve next time. This method helps desensitize your anxiety and builds a portfolio of successful experiences that boost your confidence.

Visual Element: Anxiety Trigger Chart

To aid in identifying and managing your triggers, consider creating an Anxiety Trigger Chart. Use a simple table or graph to list everyday situations that are anxiety-inducing. Next to each situation, note the level of anxiety you typically feel on a scale from 1 to 10, and jot down any specific thoughts or fears associated with that scenario. This visual tool can help you recognize patterns in your anxiety triggers and serve as a reference point for applying cognitive restructuring techniques.

By combining these cognitive and physical strategies with gradual exposure, you can significantly reduce the impact of social anxiety on your life. While the process requires persistence and may involve temporarily facing uncomfortable feelings, the freedom it brings to your social interactions and overall well-being is a worthy reward. As you continue to apply these techniques, remember that each step forward, no matter how small, is crucial to building a more confident and composed version of yourself.

3.3 Breaking Through Small Talk to Meaningful Dialogue

Small talk is often the gateway to more significant, meaningful exchanges. It's like the shallow end of a swimming pool—where you first get your feet wet before plunging into the deep end. Small talk about the weather, recent news, or the day's events might seem trivial, but it plays a crucial role in building rapport and setting a comfortable tone for what follows. This initial chitchat helps gauge the other person's mood and openness to conversation, providing a non-threatening way to initiate contact. You can transform casual interactions into opportunities for deeper connection and understanding by mastering the transition from small talk to more substantial dialogue.

Transitioning effectively from small talk to more meaningful conversation is an art that involves recognizing and acting upon verbal and non-verbal cues. An essential technique is actively listening during the initial light-hearted exchange to pick up on topics that might interest both parties more personally. For instance, if someone mentions enjoying a recent vacation, you might use this as a bridge to ask about their experiences with different cultures or their travel bucket list. This shifts the conversation from generic to personal and shows that you are paying attention to what they share, which can make the other person feel valued and understood.

Another bridging technique involves offering personal information related to the small talk topic but leading to a broader discussion area. For example, suppose the conversation begins with a discussion of a popular TV show. In that case, you might share an insight about how the show's themes relate to a broader social issue, inviting the other person to explore the topic more deeply. This method can smoothly shift the focus of the conversation from surface-level to more significant matters without seeming forced or abrupt.

Open-ended questions are invaluable tools for deepening conversations. They require more than a yes-or-no answer and encourage others to share their thoughts and feelings more. Questions like "What inspired your interest in this field?" or "How do you think we can address this issue in our community?" prompt reflection and detailed responses. These questions show interest in the other person's opinions and experiences, fostering a dialogue that can lead to a deeper understanding and connection.

Active engagement in the conversation is crucial for encouraging deeper dialogue. This means showing genuine interest in what the other person is saying through verbal affirmations like "That sounds fascinating; tell me more" or non-verbal cues such as nodding and maintaining eye contact. By being fully present in the conversation, you signal to the other person that their views and experiences are essential to you, making them feel appreciated and more willing to open up. This level of engagement enriches the conversation and strengthens the relationship, building a foundation of trust and mutual respect that can encourage even more intimate exchanges in the future.

By understanding the role of small talk in building rapport, mastering the art of transitioning to deeper topics, employing open-ended questions, and engaging actively in the conversation, you equip yourself with the tools to turn everyday interactions into meaningful dialogues. These skills are invaluable in personal relationships and professional settings, where connecting with others on a deeper level can lead to better teamwork, more innovative collaborations, and a more harmonious work environment. As you continue to practice these techniques, you'll find that what starts as simple small talk can lead to rich, fulfilling, and illuminating conversations, opening doors to new perspectives and deeper connections.

3.4 Overcoming Cultural Barriers in Communication

In our interconnected world, the ability to communicate across cultural boundaries is not just an advantage but a necessity. Understanding different cultures' varied communication styles, norms, and taboos is paramount to avoiding misunderstandings that impede personal and professional relationships. Imagine you're presenting a business proposal to a group of international stakeholders. Without an awareness of their cultural contexts, a single misinterpreted gesture or poorly chosen word could jeopardize your entire endeavor. This is where cultural awareness steps in—it involves a deep understanding of how people from different cultural backgrounds interpret messages, express themselves, and perceive the world around them.

Building cultural awareness begins with education and exposure. Reading about different cultures, their histories, and social norms provides a foundational understanding that can be crucial in anticipating how your actions and words might be perceived. However, actual cultural competence often comes from direct exposure to diverse groups. This could be through travel, where you experience different cultures first-hand, or local experiences like attending cultural festivals, workshops, or even joining community groups that expose you to various cultural perspectives. Such immersive experiences allow you to see the world through others' eyes, increasing your empathy and improving your ability to communicate effectively across cultural divides.

Cultural sensitivity training is another vital tool in this learning process. Many organizations now offer workshops and training sessions to enhance workplace cultural sensitivity. These programs typically cover common cultural misunderstandings, strategies for effective multicultural communication, and ways to resolve cross-cultural conflicts. They also often include practical role-playing exercises that allow participants to experience the challenges and rewards of intercultural communication first-hand. Engaging in these training opportunities broadens your understanding and equips you with practical skills that can be directly applied in your day-to-day interactions.

Regarding practical tips for cross-cultural communication, clarity and simplicity are your best allies. In conversations with people from different backgrounds, it's wise to use clear, simple language free of idioms, slang, or cultural references that might not translate well. This helps ensure your message is understood, regardless of the listener's cultural background. Being mindful of nonverbal cues is equally essential. Something as simple as a nod can vary in meaning from one culture to another—in some cultures, it signifies agreement, while in others, it might simply mean that someone is listening. Observing these subtle nonverbal cues and asking for clarification can prevent potential misunderstandings.

Success in cross-cultural communication is often highlighted by stories of individuals and organizations that have effectively bridged the cultural divide. Consider the case of a tech startup that successfully expanded its operations to Asia by implementing a robust cultural training program for its employees. Before the expansion, the company invested in language training and cultural workshops focusing on business etiquette, negotiation styles, and communication preferences in the target countries. This preparation paid off— the company avoided common cultural pitfalls and built strong relationships with local partners, leading to a successful market entry. These success stories serve as powerful reminders of the importance of cultural competence and the potential for enriched relationships and opportunities that come with it.

By cultivating a deep understanding of cultural differences, actively seeking opportunities for cultural exposure and sensitivity training, and applying practical communication strategies, you can confidently navigate the complexities of cross-cultural communication. This enhances your interactions and opens up a world of professional opportunities, enabling you to connect and collaborate with people from all walks of life. As you continue to engage with diverse cultures, remember that each interaction is an opportunity to expand your horizons, enrich your experiences, and build bridges across the vast and varied landscape of human culture.

3.5 Dealing with Difficult Conversations Gracefully

Navigating difficult conversations is akin to walking a tightrope. Balance is crucial; too much emotion can lead to conflict, while too little may seem insincere. Whether it's a disagreement with a friend, delivering critical feedback at work, or discussing a sensitive topic, these conversations require a diplomatic approach. Preparation is your first tool in handling these scenarios effectively. Start by clearly defining your intentions for the conversation. What is your goal? You may need to resolve a misunderstanding, provide feedback, or discuss a delicate subject. A clear objective will guide your discussion and help keep the conversation on track.

Additionally, adopting a constructive mindset is vital. Approach the conversation to understand and be understood rather than to win an argument. This frame of mind fosters a cooperative rather than confrontational atmosphere, which can lead to more productive outcomes.

Emotional regulation is another critical component in managing difficult conversations. Emotions can run high during challenging interactions, making it easy to react impulsively. To maintain your composure, practice techniques such as taking deep, slow breaths to calm your nervous system and allow yourself a moment to collect your thoughts. This simple act can help prevent the conversation from escalating. Staying focused on the topic at hand is also crucial. Avoid veering into irrelevant personal attacks or dredging up past grievances, which can divert the conversation and increase tensions.

The language you choose plays a significant role in the tone and outcome of the discussion. To foster clarity and reduce defensiveness, use "I" statements rather than "you" statements. For example, saying "I feel frustrated when meetings start late" is less accusatory and more likely to be received well than "You are always late to meetings." Additionally, strive to keep your descriptions neutral and factual. This approach helps de-escalate emotions by focusing on observable facts rather than subjective interpretations.

Finally, how you recover from and follow up on a difficult conversation can impact your relationship moving forward. Reflect on what went well and what could have been handled better. This reflection can be an invaluable learning experience, helping you improve your communication skills. Consider mending and strengthening the relationship if the conversation was not planned. This might involve apologizing for any part of the conversation where you were at fault or suggesting another talk to clarify unresolved issues. Following up shows your commitment to the relationship and willingness to work through challenges, which can help rebuild trust and understanding.

In sum, by preparing with clear intentions, adopting a constructive mindset, practicing emotional regulation, using effective language, and thoughtfully recovering from difficult conversations, you equip yourself with a robust toolkit for handling these challenges gracefully. These strategies make you a better communicator and strengthen your relationships as you navigate conflicts with respect and understanding.

As we conclude this chapter on overcoming communication barriers, we reflect on the journey from understanding personal communication styles and managing anxiety to enhancing dialogue and navigating cultural differences. Each section builds on the last, equipping you with the skills to face and thrive through communication challenges. Looking ahead, the next chapter will detail ways of refining your advanced conversation skills, where we will explore persuasive techniques, negotiation strategies, and the art of impactful storytelling. These skills will further enhance your ability to communicate effectively in personal and professional contexts, preparing you for various communicative encounters.

4

ADVANCED CONVERSATION SKILLS

Imagine you're at a crossroads in a lively city center, observing people from all walks of life converging and diverging, each participant in a grand, unspoken dance. Here, every gesture and every word holds the potential to lead to new paths or close doors. This is the complex world of advanced conversation skills, where the art of persuasion, the subtleties of trust, and the nuances of social influence come into play. This chapter explores these sophisticated aspects of communication, empowering you to navigate and actively shape the interactions that fill your daily life.

4.1 Mastering the Art of Persuasion in Everyday Conversations

Understanding Persuasion

At its core, persuasion is the art of influencing or convincing others to embrace a point of view, adopt a behavior, or accept a decision. Unlike manipulation, which involves deceit or exploitation, ethical persuasion respects the autonomy and dignity of all parties involved. It is a foundational skill that enhances interactions in every aspect of life, from negotiating raises to convincing your child to do their homework. Persuasion operates under the premise that by presenting compelling arguments, evoking relevant emotions, and demonstrating credibility, you can encourage others to see a situation from your perspective and potentially agree with your conclusions.

Principles of Persuasion

Dr. Robert Cialdini's six principles of persuasion provide a psychological blueprint for effective influence. These principles—reciprocity, consistency, social proof, authority, liking, and scarcity—are rooted in the basic tendencies of human behavior. For instance, reciprocity compels us to return favors, while consistency drives us to align our actions with our commitments and beliefs. Social proof leverages the power of group dynamics, suggesting that we are more likely to engage in behaviors endorsed by others. Authority emphasizes the sway of credible experts, whereas liking points to the simple truth that we are more easily persuaded by people we like. Lastly, scarcity capitalizes on our fear of missing out, highlighting an opportunity's unique benefits and exclusive advantages.

These principles can be ethically integrated into daily conversations to enhance your persuasive impact. For example, when trying to encourage a team at work to adopt a new process, you might start by highlighting how similar teams (social proof) have successfully implemented the change, offer a small incentive (reciprocity) to the early adopters, and present yourself as someone knowledgeable and experienced (authority) in this new method.

Building Credibility and Trust

The effectiveness of your persuasion hinges significantly on your credibility and the trust you inspire in others. Credibility stems from your expertise and the consistency of your behavior, while trust is cultivated through transparency, empathy, and integrity. To build these elements, focus on communicating clearly and openly, showing genuine concern for the interests of others, and consistently delivering on your promises. For instance, if you commit to following up on a colleague's request, doing so promptly reinforces your reliability and strengthens their trust in your words and actions.

One effective way to enhance your credibility is to admit when you don't have all the answers. This honesty can paradoxically increase your persuasiveness by boosting your trustworthiness. It shows that you are more committed to truth than to maintaining an appearance of infallibility.

Practical Persuasion Scenarios

Real-life applications of persuasion are as varied as the situations you encounter daily. Consider a scenario in which you must convince your family to adopt healthier eating habits. By explaining the benefits (authority), showing testimonials from other families who have seen positive health results (social proof), and perhaps introducing a tasty but healthy new meal each week (liking), you can more effectively persuade your loved ones to make a change. In a professional context, suppose you must convince your manager to invest in new software. Demonstrating its efficiency with a trial run (reciprocity), aligning it with the company's goals (consistency), and highlighting limited-time offers from the software provider (scarcity) can significantly enhance your persuasive appeal.

Visual Element: Persuasion Techniques Chart

To further help understand and apply these principles, consider this chart that outlines each of Cialdini's principles, along with a brief description and a practical example of how it can be used in everyday conversations. This visual guide is a handy reference for quickly recalling and implementing effective persuasion tactics in various social and professional situations.

By MASTERING PERSUASION, you equip yourself to influence outcomes and inspire change positively and ethically. Whether engaging in family discussions, navigating workplace dynamics, or participating in community initiatives, the principles and techniques explored here can enhance your effectiveness as a communicator, allowing you to achieve your objectives while respecting and valuing the perspectives of others. As you continue to apply these insights, you'll find that your conversations are not just exchanges of information but pivotal interactions that shape the fabric of your daily interactions and long-term relationships.

4.2 Negotiation Skills for the Reluctant Communicator

Negotiation is an essential skill, not just for business leaders and diplomats but for anyone who ever needs to reach an agreement with another party. Negotiation involves two or more parties with something the other wants, striving to achieve an acceptable consensus. Understanding the basics of negotiation, including critical concepts like BATNA and ZOPA, is crucial. BATNA, or Best Alternative to a Negotiated Agreement, is your backup plan if the negotiation fails. Knowing your BATNA is vital because it gives you an alternative path and helps prevent desperation; you know you have options, which typically strengthens your negotiating position. ZOPA, or Zone of Possible Agreement, represents the range within which an agreement satisfies both parties. It's the overlap between what one party is willing to accept and what the other party is willing to give. Identifying the ZOPA is critical as it helps determine whether a deal is possible and guides the direction of the negotiations.

Preparing for negotiation is as essential as the negotiation itself. Preparation involves setting clear goals, understanding the other party's needs, and scenario planning. Begin by defining what success looks like for you: what are your most essential needs, and what are you willing to compromise on? Equally important is understanding the goals and pressures facing the other party. This empathy can provide significant leverage during the negotiation, as you can propose solutions that meet their needs and yours. Scenario planning involves thinking through different ways the negotiation could unfold and preparing for each possibility. This not only helps in staying calm during the talks but also in being flexible and adaptive as new information and circumstances arise.

Specific negotiation techniques can be particularly effective for those anxious about confrontations. Using open-ended questions helps engage the other party in a dialogue, drawing out their preferences and priorities without confrontation. Active listening is another essential skill; by genuinely paying attention to what the other party is saying and reflecting their messages back to them, you gain valuable information and build rapport and trust. Framing offers win-win solutions that can alleviate much of the stress associated with negotiation, shifting the focus from competing over resources to collaborating on mutually beneficial outcomes. For instance, if negotiating a job offer, instead of simply asking for a higher salary, you could propose a development plan that includes professional training that benefits both you and the employer in the long term.

Managing negotiation anxiety is crucial for effective communication. Many people feel nervous about negotiations because they fear conflict or are worried about the outcome. However, understanding that nervousness is a normal part of any challenging conversation can help manage these feelings. Preparation is critical to reducing anxiety; the more you prepare, the more confident you will feel. Practice also plays a crucial role. Engaging in mock negotiations or role-playing with friends or colleagues can help you get used to negotiation dynamics. This practice can demystify the process and reduce anxiety by familiarizing you with negotiating tactics and responses.

Additionally, pacing yourself during the negotiation can prevent overwhelming feelings. If you feel anxiety building up, don't hesitate to request a break to compose yourself. This helps manage your stress and gives you time to reassess your strategy and next steps.

Incorporating these strategies into your negotiation approach can transform your experience from daunting to empowering. Whether you're discussing terms with a potential employer, resolving conflicts with a partner, or simply deciding where to dine with friends, these skills are invaluable. They enhance your ability to achieve favorable outcomes and build confidence in handling discussions that require give and take. As you continue to practice and refine these techniques, you'll find that what once seemed like a stressful ordeal can become an opportunity for collaboration and mutual satisfaction.

4.3 Conflict Resolution: Keeping Cool and Finding Solutions

Conflict is as natural to human relationships as breathing. Whether it arises from miscommunications, conflicting interests, or differing perspectives, understanding how to manage and resolve conflict is crucial for maintaining healthy personal and professional relationships. The first step towards effective conflict resolution is identifying the sources of conflict. Conflicts arise from resource constraints, personality clashes, unmet expectations, or misaligned goals. For example, a team might experience conflict in the workplace due to competition for limited resources such as budget or workforce. In personal relationships, conflicts often stem from unmet emotional needs or expectations that have not been communicated. Recognizing the underlying causes of conflicts can provide a more straightforward pathway to resolving them and preventing similar issues.

Effective communication strategies are vital once you've identified the source of the conflict. Techniques such as using I-statements play a crucial role in de-escalating conflicts. I-statements allow you to express your feelings and needs without blaming the other party, which can help keep defenses low and dialogue open. For instance, instead of saying, "You never listen to me," you could say, "I feel unheard when I talk about my day, and you don't seem to respond." This approach communicates how you feel and does so in a way that is less likely to provoke a defensive response. Ensuring all parties feel heard is another critical aspect of conflict resolution. Active listening, where you genuinely focus on understanding the other person's perspective without planning your rebuttal, can help validate their feelings and build mutual understanding. This validation is often the key to transforming a confrontational conversation into a cooperative discussion focused on finding solutions.

Problem-solving approaches in conflict resolution include mediation, compromise, and collaboration. Mediation involves a neutral third party who helps facilitate a solution by ensuring that each party's views are equally heard and understood. This can be particularly effective when emotions run high and communication has broken down. Compromise requires each party to give up something to reach a mutually acceptable solution. It's often used when time constraints or external pressures demand a quick resolution. However, the most sustainable method is collaboration, where parties work together to find a win-win solution that satisfies everyone's needs. This approach not only resolves the immediate conflict but can also strengthen relationships by building trust and goodwill.

Managing relationships post-conflict is crucial for healing and preventing future issues. This involves openly discussing what each party has learned from the experience, adjusting behaviors or processes as needed, and reaffirming commitment to the relationship. Recognizing and appreciating each party's effort to resolve the conflict is also essential. Such acknowledgments can reinforce positive interactions and communication patterns, making managing future disputes easier. Regular check-ins can help ensure that the relationship remains positive and that minor grievances are addressed before they escalate into significant conflicts. This proactive communication fosters an environment where openness and honesty are valued, laying a solid foundation for enduring personal and professional relationships.

Understanding the roots of conflict, utilizing effective communication techniques, and employing problem-solving strategies can help you confidently navigate its complexities. This resolves immediate issues and enhances your ability to foster and maintain healthy, resilient relationships. Whether at home, among friends, or in the workplace, these skills are indispensable tools that empower you to handle disputes constructively and collaboratively, paving the way for more harmonious interactions and stronger connections.

4.4 Storytelling Techniques to Captivate and Engage

Storytelling is an ancient art form, weaving images and ideas into a tapestry that engages and inspires. Stories can captivate and influence, whether around a campfire, within a bustling café, or during a high-powered corporate meeting. Understanding the fundamental elements of effective storytelling—structure, character, conflict, and resolution—is crucial for anyone looking to enhance their communicative prowess. A well-told story follows a clear structure that guides the audience through a beginning, where the setting and characters are introduced; a middle, where conflicts and challenges build tension; and an end, where a resolution brings closure. Each element hooks the listener's attention and pulls them into the story's world.

Characters are the heart of any story. They are the vessels through which your audience forms emotional connections, rooting for them, fearing for them, and engaging with their journeys. Developing relatable, three-dimensional characters involves showing their strengths, vulnerabilities, hopes, and fears. This connection makes your audience care about what happens next, which is why character development should always be noticed. Conflict, meanwhile, is the engine of your story. It introduces the central challenge or problem that the characters must navigate. This could range from external conflicts like adversarial forces or natural disasters to internal conflicts such as emotional turmoil or ethical dilemmas. The resolution, then, is how these conflicts are ultimately addressed. It provides a satisfying conclusion to the story, resolving the tension and answering the central question posed by the narrative.

Connecting emotionally with your audience is essential for a story's lasting impact. This emotional engagement can be achieved through vivid imagery and relatable experiences. Descriptive language that appeals to the senses can transport listeners to the story's setting, allowing them to see, hear, and feel the world you're describing. Relatable experiences reflecting universal truths or everyday struggles ensure your story resonates more deeply with your audience. They see parts of themselves in your tale, which can be comforting and compelling. For example, a story about overcoming adversity, with precise sensory details and universal emotions, can inspire and motivate, making the narrative stick long after the story has ended.

Adapting storytelling techniques to different contexts is another layer of this craft. In professional presentations, your stories must be concise and directly related to your business objectives, using relatable characters and scenarios to underline key points. In casual conversations, stories can be more personal, using humor and anecdotes to build social bonds. Written communications often allow for more detailed storytelling, providing the space to develop complex characters and intricate plots that would be too elaborate for spoken word. Understanding the demands and opportunities of each context ensures that your stories are heard and effective in achieving their intended purpose.

Practicing storytelling is vital. Engaging in storytelling workshops can provide valuable opportunities to hone your skills. These workshops often involve direct feedback from storytelling experts and peers, which can help refine your technique and delivery. Additionally, digital platforms that allow for storytelling, such as blogs or social media, can be excellent places to practice. These platforms provide a space to share your stories and offer feedback from a broader audience. This type of engagement can be incredibly beneficial for developing an authentic and appealing style.

By understanding the elements of a good story, connecting with your audience on an emotional level, adapting your tales to fit various contexts, and practicing regularly, you can master the art of storytelling. This skill enriches your personal and professional life and enhances your communication ability. Whether aiming to educate, entertain, persuade, or connect, storytelling is a powerful tool that can engage your listeners and leave a lasting impression when wielded with expertise and empathy.

4.5 Humor: When and How to Use It Effectively

Humor is often the glue in social interactions, a universal language that transcends boundaries, and a tool that can turn tense moments into shared experiences of joy. Yet, effectively wielding humor in communication requires finesse, as its impact heavily depends on context, timing, and the relationships between those involved. Understanding humor consists in recognizing its potential to both connect and divide. In the best scenarios, humor fosters camaraderie, eases tension, and humanizes our interactions. It can make information more memorable and help navigate difficult conversations by providing a lighter tone that facilitates openness. However, humor also carries risks; it can easily be misinterpreted, alienate, or offend if used insensitively. Therefore, appreciating the power of humor and knowing when and how to employ it are crucial skills in effective communication.

There are several types of humor, each with its own charm and appropriate context. Situational humor arises from the circumstances or environment and often involves a witty observation that highlights the absurdity or irony of the situation. This humor is particularly effective in day-to-day interactions where shared experiences can be highlighted to create a bond. Self-deprecating humor, where the speaker makes fun of themselves, can be helpful to show vulnerability and approachability, making you seem more relatable and less threatening, especially in leadership or public speaking roles. However, it requires a careful balance to avoid undermining your credibility or authority. Observational humor involves making humorous remarks about everyday life. This form is widely appreciated because it resonates with everyday experiences but demands a keen sense of timing and audience receptivity to avoid sounding contrived or irrelevant.

Incorporating humor into your conversations involves a keen awareness of the audience and the setting. Timing is critical; humor must feel spontaneous and relevant to the discussion. It's also essential to consider your audience's cultural and social context to ensure the humor will be understood and appreciated rather than causing confusion or offense. For instance, humor in a professional presentation can lighten the mood and improve engagement, but it should be relevant to the material and respectful of the audience's diversity. The humor should enhance the content and not distract from the important messages you wish to convey.

Engaging with a wide range of comedic styles can be incredibly beneficial to develop your sense of humor. Watching comedies, reading humorous books, and listening to comedy podcasts are excellent ways to expose yourself to different types of humor and comedic timing. Note what makes you laugh and why, observing how comedians build up a joke and deliver the punchline. Practicing joke delivery in safe environments, like among close friends or family, can help you gauge reactions and refine your timing and delivery. It's a process of trial and error; not every joke will land, and that's okay. Each interaction provides valuable feedback on your comedic sense and helps you understand better what works and what doesn't in various social contexts.

Incorporating humor into your communication arsenal can transform your interactions, making them more engaging and enjoyable. Understanding the types of humor and learning to use them appropriately can enhance your relatability and effectiveness as a communicator, ensuring that your humor brings smiles rather than frowns.

As this chapter on advanced conversation skills closes, we reflect on the journey through the art of persuasion, negotiation techniques, conflict resolution, and the engaging power of storytelling and humor. Each section has built upon the last, equipping you with a sophisticated toolkit to enhance your interactions and forge deeper connections. Looking ahead, the next chapter will explore the dynamics of personal relationships, where these advanced skills will be applied to deepen bonds and navigate the complexities of closer, more personal interactions. Here, the principles of effective communication meet the heart of human relationships, paving the way for more meaningful and enduring connections.

5

———————

BUILDING PROFESSIONAL RELATIONSHIPS

Imagine entering a grand hall filled with potential mentors, collaborators, and friends. This is not just any gathering; it's a crucible of opportunities that could shape your professional future. Networking, often misconceived as a series of calculated interactions, is about crafting genuine connections woven into your career's fabric. In this chapter, we will navigate the nuanced landscape of networking, debunking myths and laying out strategies that transform it from a daunting task into an enriching experience. Networking can open doors to unexpected and beneficial professional relationships, whether at a bustling conference or during a casual coffee meet-up.

5.1 Networking Made Easy: Simple Steps to Connect

Understanding Networking

Networking is an essential ingredient in the recipe for professional success. However, it often carries a stigma—an image of awkward interactions and self-serving exchanges. Let's dismantle this misconception: effective networking isn't about collecting business cards or crafting a perfect sales pitch. It's about finding common ground, sharing ideas, and fostering mutual support. It serves as a bridge that connects you to opportunities that are not always visible or accessible through traditional channels. Studies have shown that many job opportunities are never advertised but are filled through networking. This hidden job market can only be tapped through connections made from genuine engagement and mutual interest.

Preparation for Networking Events

Preparation is vital before attending any networking event. Start by researching the attendees and speakers. This knowledge will boost your confidence and enable you to tailor your conversations to resonate with the interests and needs of those you meet. Set clear objectives for what you want to achieve—gaining insights into a new industry, seeking job opportunities, or finding a mentor. Having specific goals in mind will help you navigate the event more effectively and measure your success afterward.

Effective Networking Techniques

At the heart of networking lies the art of conversation. Initiating dialogue can be as simple as commenting on a shared experience or asking open-ended questions about the event's theme. Remember, the goal is to ignite meaningful discussions that could lead to deeper professional relationships. Business cards, while traditional, still play a crucial role. They provide a tangible reminder of your encounter and a direct way to share your contact information. However, the digital age has expanded networking tools to include social media platforms. LinkedIn, for example, can be a powerful tool for pre-event connections and post-event follow-ups. Engage with attendees and speakers through thoughtful comments or shared content to maintain the momentum of your newly formed connections.

5.2 The Follow-Up: Ensuring Your Connections Last

The real magic of networking doesn't end when you leave the room; it begins. Picture this: you've made a great impression, exchanged contacts, and shared ideas with promising professionals. Now, the crucial part is the follow-up. This step transforms fleeting encounters into lasting professional relationships that can significantly impact your career trajectory. The art of following up is both a strategy and a courtesy, showing that you value the connection and are interested in nurturing it.

Think of each new contact as a seed you've planted. Without proper care—water, sunlight, and nutrients—it won't grow. Similarly, without a thoughtful follow-up, the initial connection may fail to develop into a robust network link. The optimal follow-up time is 24-48 hours after your first meeting. This promptness ensures that the interaction is fresh in both parties' minds, making your message more relevant and impactful. As for the methods, they can vary based on the context of your meeting and the preferences of your new contact. A thank-you email is a universally accepted approach and is appreciated for its professionalism and convenience. For a more personal touch, a LinkedIn message can reinforce your new connection on a platform dedicated to professional networking. When a stronger personal connection is established, a phone call can convey more engaged interest and commitment to the relationship.

Crafting your follow-up message requires a delicate balance of courtesy, relevance, and brevity. Start by expressing your appreciation for the time spent and the conversation you had. This sets a positive tone and shows your gratitude and professionalism. Next, reiterate any mutual interests or specific topics discussed. For instance, if you both shared enthusiasm about a recent industry development, mention this in your follow-up. This reinforces the connection, showing that you were engaged during the conversation and are invested in the topics that matter to you. Proposing a next step is crucial; suggest a concrete action that moves the relationship forward, such as meeting for coffee to discuss a collaborative idea or attending a relevant event together. This shows initiative and helps transition the relationship from a casual encounter to a purposeful connection.

Maintaining the relationship over time is where your networking efforts come to fruition. Regular check-ins via email or social media keep the conversation and your connection active. Sharing articles, videos, or events that align with their interests can add value to their professional life, showing that you're thoughtful and resourceful. Inviting them to webinars, meetups, or industry events strengthens your professional relationship and provides ongoing face-to-face interactions and collaboration opportunities. These consistent, value-adding interactions are critical to a dynamic, supportive professional network that grows and evolves with your career.

By mastering the follow-up and nurturing your professional relationships with regular, meaningful interactions, you ensure that your network is not just a collection of names in a contact list but a vibrant community of collaborators, mentors, and friends who are invested in mutual success. These connections form the backbone of your professional support system, offering advice, partnership, and opportunities for years to come. As you continue to engage with your network, remember that the strength of your relationships often determines the height of your achievements.

5.3 Communicating Up: Talking to Bosses and Higher-Ups

Navigating the intricacies of hierarchical dynamics in the workplace requires skill and a keen understanding of the subtleties involved in communicating upward. When you speak with superiors, every element, from the tone of your voice to the timing of your input, plays a critical role in how your message is received. Recognizing the importance of these elements can transform your interactions from routine exchanges into opportunities for career advancement and personal growth. The art of communicating up is not about currying favor; instead, it's about demonstrating your professionalism, insight, and value to the organization respectfully and effectively.

When addressing those higher up in the organizational hierarchy, the tone of your communication should strike a balance between professionalism and confidence. It's crucial to convey respect not just through the words you choose but also through your delivery. This respect is demonstrated by acknowledging their experience and position without undermining your contributions. Timing, too, is pivotal. Choosing the right moment to present ideas or concerns can mean the difference between being heard and being overlooked. For instance, proposing a new project idea during a crisis moment might not receive the attention it deserves, whereas timing it for a period of strategic planning could spotlight its relevance and your foresight.

Content, the core of your communication, must be well-considered and relevant. When preparing to speak with a superior, focus on clarity and conciseness. Refrain from cluttering your message with unnecessary details that can dilute its impact. Instead, distill your message to its essence while ensuring it remains informative and backed by data whenever possible. For example, if you are proposing a new efficiency-enhancing tool, be ready with specific data on how much time and resources it can save and potential ROI, which directly addresses likely concerns and questions from your superiors.

Strategies for Effective Upward Communication

Effective upward communication also involves being proactive about feedback. Superiors often have insights that can help you refine your approach and enhance your projects, but their feedback can sometimes be curt or challenging. Learning to receive and respond to feedback constructively is a crucial skill. Start by listening actively to the input without interrupting, which shows respect and openness to growth. When you respond, do so thoughtfully. Asking clarifying questions can help you understand the feedback fully and demonstrate that you are engaged and committed to improvement. For example, if feedback on a report you wrote was "too detailed," you might ask, "Can you point to a section where you felt the detail was unnecessary?" This shows that you are willing to consider their perspective and work on specific areas of improvement.

Moreover, demonstrating appreciation for feedback—even when it's tough—can set you apart as a resilient and adaptable professional. A simple "Thank you for that insight. I'll incorporate it moving forward" can affirm that you value their guidance and are eager to evolve.

Advocating for Yourself

Advocating for yourself in discussions with superiors is another facet of effective upward communication. This involves expressing your needs, achievements, and aspirations clearly and professionally. For instance, being your advocate during performance reviews or project proposals is essential. Presenting data and achievements can substantiate your contributions and highlight your professional impact. If you led a team that completed a project under budget and ahead of schedule, bring these metrics into your review discussions. Such data quantifies your accomplishments and frames your discussion in terms of tangible benefits to the organization.

In advocating for yourself, it's also beneficial to articulate your career aspirations and seek advice on achieving them. This can open up opportunities for mentorship and guidance. Expressing your professional goals and asking for input shows initiative and invites your superiors to invest in your growth. For example, you might say, "I am very interested in moving into a managerial role in the next few years. What skills should I focus on developing to prepare for this transition?"

By mastering these nuanced elements of communicating up—understanding the dynamics of hierarchy, choosing the right tone, timing, and content, handling feedback constructively, and effectively advocating for yourself—you enhance your professional relationships and foster a reputation as a thoughtful, proactive, and resilient professional. These skills are about making an impression, building lasting professional respect, and positioning yourself for continual growth and success within your career.

5.4 Team Communication: Ensuring Clarity and Cohesion

In the synergy of a team, transparent and open communication acts as the lifeblood that maintains the health and effectiveness of group interactions. It's not just about exchanging information; it's about building an environment where trust and team cohesion are at the forefront, paving the way for collaborative success. When teams foster open communication, they set a foundation where trust can flourish. Trust, in this context, is not merely about believing that your colleagues will complete their tasks. It's about feeling confident to express ideas, questions, and concerns without fear of dismissal or ridicule. This level of trust is cultivated through consistent and clear communication, where each team member feels heard and valued.

Encouraging a communicative team environment begins with leadership. Leaders must model the communication behaviors they expect to see within their teams. This could mean being transparent about team goals, challenges, and the rationale behind certain decisions. When leaders articulate these elements clearly and openly, team members are more likely to reciprocate this transparency in their day-to-day interactions, contributing to a culture where information flows freely and effectively. Regular team meetings are a practical tool in this endeavor. These gatherings provide a structured forum for sharing updates, brainstorming solutions, and addressing concerns. However, the effectiveness of these meetings often hinges on their execution. An agenda can help maintain focus and efficiency, ensuring that each meeting delivers value and reinforces the importance of each team member's contributions.

In today's digital age, the tools we use to communicate are just as significant as what we communicate. Shared digital platforms like project management software can enhance team communication by providing a transparent, accessible space where progress can be tracked and updates can be shared seamlessly. These tools often have features like comment sections, task assignments, and progress indicators, which help keep everyone on the same page and moving towards common goals. Clear documentation is another pillar of effective team communication. Documenting processes, decisions, and agreements helps minimize misunderstandings and provides a reliable reference to which team members can return when needed. This practice not only aids in maintaining clarity but also ensures continuity in projects, especially when there are changes in team composition.

If left unresolved, miscommunications can become a source of ongoing conflict and diminished team productivity. Practical techniques for addressing miscommunications are, therefore, crucial. One helpful approach is the clarification process, where team members are encouraged to discuss their understanding of the tasks or issues openly. This can involve restating the information received and confirming its accuracy before acting on it. When miscommunications are identified, addressing them promptly prevents the compounding of errors and potential frustrations. Regular feedback loops can also play a significant role in identifying and resolving misunderstandings. By creating a regular schedule for feedback—both formal and informal—teams can ensure ongoing opportunities to correct course and refine their communication practices.

Fostering an environment that encourages open dialogue is essential for tapping into the diverse perspectives within a team. The team is richer when members from different backgrounds and viewpoints feel encouraged to share their thoughts. Techniques to promote this kind of openness include using inclusive language that respects all team members, structuring meetings to allow equal participation opportunities, and explicitly asking for input from quieter team members who might otherwise remain on the sidelines. Additionally, creating smaller breakout groups during larger meetings can encourage participation from individuals who may not feel comfortable speaking up in a large setting. These smaller groups can then share their discussions with the larger team, ensuring all voices are heard and considered.

By implementing these strategies—building a foundation of trust through open communication, utilizing practical tools and practices, swiftly addressing miscommunications, and encouraging a culture of open dialogue—teams can achieve cohesion and clarity that propels them toward collective success. As you continue to engage with your team, remember that each interaction is an opportunity to strengthen these dynamics, creating a work environment that not only fosters productivity but also supports and values the contributions of every team member.

5.5 Email Etiquette: Communicating Effectively in Writing

In the digital age, email remains a cornerstone of professional communication, as a bridge connecting us across continents and time zones in mere seconds. Yet, its convenience does not negate the need for meticulous attention to its use. Professionals should write straightforward emails, maintain professionalism, and respect the recipient's time. Let's examine the principles of crafting effective emails, guiding you to communicate with precision and tact, and ensuring your messages are not just sent but well-received and understood.

The essence of professional email writing can be distilled into three core principles: clarity, brevity, and professionalism. Clarity involves being concise in your language and direct in your messaging. Each email should have a clear purpose or action item, making it easy for the recipient to understand your intentions and respond appropriately. Brevity relates to the length of your email. Time is a precious commodity, and respecting the recipient's time by keeping your message concise demonstrates consideration and increases the likelihood of your email being read and addressed promptly. Email professionalism is about maintaining a tone that reflects respect and formality appropriate to the workplace. This includes using a polite greeting, a respectful sign-off, and ensuring that the body of your email avoids slang and overly casual language, which can undermine the seriousness of your message.

Structure of a Professional Email

A well-structured email serves as a framework that guides the recipient through your message efficiently and effectively. Start with a subject line that is direct and informative. This line sets the expectation and relevance of the email, such as "Request for Budget Report Feedback by EOD." Following the subject line, your email should begin with a professional greeting, either a generic greeting like

"Dear [Name]" or a more personalized one if you have an established relationship with the recipient. The body of your email is where clarity and brevity are paramount. Begin with a sentence that states the purpose of your email, followed by supporting details or requests. Be direct and upfront about what you are asking or what information you are providing. Conclude your email with a call to action or a summary of the steps needed, ensuring there is no ambiguity about what is expected moving forward. Sign off with a professional closing, such as "Best regards" or "Sincerely," followed by your name and any necessary contact information or titles.

Tone and Style Appropriateness

Adjusting the tone and style of your email is crucial and should reflect the nature of your relationship with the recipient and the email's purpose. For more formal interactions, or when emailing someone for the first time, it's advisable to err on the side of formality in tone and language. As familiarity and rapport build, the tone of your emails can adapt to become more relaxed, though still maintaining professionalism. Additionally, the purpose of your email should guide its style. For instance, an email conveying company-wide policy changes will have a more formal tone than an email organizing a casual team lunch.

Common Email Pitfalls to Avoid

Several common pitfalls can undermine the effectiveness of your email communication. The overuse of jargon and complex language can obscure the clarity of your message, especially when communicating with recipients from different fields or industries. Keep your language simple. Avoiding proofreading is another frequent oversight leading to spelling, grammar, and punctuation errors, potentially harming your professional credibility. Please take a moment to review your email before sending it. Another mistake is being too casual in emails, especially in professional contexts. This can include using slang, emojis, or overly familiar language, which might be perceived as unprofessional or too informal for the situation.

By adhering to these guidelines and principles, your emails can achieve their purpose more effectively, ensuring your communication is heard, respected, and valued. As we turn to the next chapter, we'll explore digital communication in the modern world, expanding on navigating various platforms and tools that define our daily interactions in the digital sphere. This knowledge will enhance your communication skills and prepare you for the evolving landscape of professional interactions.

PLEASE SHARE!

If you believe others might benefit from reading this book, please leave a rating or a review on Amazon. If you are reading this in an ebook, please click here to be taken to the review page.

If you are reading a print book, please scan the QR code below to access the review page.

Thank you!

6

DIGITAL COMMUNICATION IN THE MODERN WORLD

I magine a world where your words have wings—flying through the digital skies, crossing continents and oceans in seconds, landing in the palm of a friend, a coworker, or a stranger. In this ever-connected age, digital communication forms the backbone of our daily personal and professional interactions. Texts, emails, social media posts, and instant messages fill our days, weaving a complex web of dialogue that shapes relationships, careers, and lives. This chapter delves into the nuanced art of digital communication, beginning with one of the most common yet intricate forms: texting. Here, the simplicity of sending a message meets the complexity of context, tone, and timing. As we explore how to navigate these waters effectively, you'll learn to use texting as a tool for conversation and as a skillful means of maintaining professionalism and warmth in your digital interactions.

6.1 Texting Tips: Keeping It Professional and Personal

Understanding Context

Recognizing when and how texting is appropriate can significantly impact the effectiveness and appropriateness of your communication. In professional scenarios, texting should be used judiciously. It is ideal for brief exchanges such as confirming meeting times or sending quick reminders. However, more complex discussions, especially those involving sensitive information, generally warrant an email or a phone call. On the other hand, personal texts allow for more flexibility and informality, providing a space for nurturing relationships with warmth and humor. The key lies in your ability to assess the situation and choose the most suitable medium and tone for your message.

Tone and Form

Maintaining a professional tone in work-related texts is crucial. This includes using complete sentences, proper grammar, and avoiding slang, which helps preserve clarity and respectfulness. For instance, a text message to a colleague saying, "Could you please send me the updated presentation by noon? Thanks!" is clear and polite. In contrast, personal texts often thrive on a lighter, more conversational tone. Letting your personality shine through is perfectly acceptable, using colloquial language and expressions reflecting your relationship with the recipient.

Response Time Etiquette

Timing can be everything in texting. Responding promptly is vital in professional contexts, as it demonstrates efficiency and respect for the sender's time. A rule of thumb is to reply within one business day, if not sooner, depending on the message's urgency. In personal settings, while immediate responses are often appreciated, they are only sometimes necessary unless the context demands it, such as planning activities or responding to specific questions. Managing expectations by communicating your availability or any delays in response can help maintain harmony and understanding in ongoing conversations.

Use of Emojis and Abbreviations

Emojis and abbreviations can add a layer of emotion or emphasis to your texts, making them more relatable and human. However, their use should be tailored to the context. In professional texts, it's generally best to use emojis sparingly and only when their meanings are clear and appropriate for the workplace. For example, a smiley face in an email to a coworker thanking them for their help can be a friendly touch, but it may not be suitable in more formal communications or with clients you do not know well. In personal communications, emojis and abbreviations can be used more freely to express emotions and bring a lively, informal tone to the conversation.

Textual Element: Texting Etiquette Checklist

To ensure your texting habits align with both professional decorum and personal warmth, consider this checklist:

- **Context Check:** Before texting, consider if this is the best medium for the message.
- **Tone Adjustment:** Match your tone to the situation—formal for professional interactions, relaxed for personal ones.
- **Grammar Matters:** Use proper spelling and grammar in professional texts.
- **Emoji Use:** Choose emojis thoughtfully, ensuring they are appropriate for the relationship and context.
- **Response Timing:** Aim to respond within an expected timeframe based on the urgency and nature of the conversation.

Mastering the art of texting in both personal and professional contexts enhances your ability to communicate effectively, helps prevent misunderstandings, and maintains the quality and professionalism of your interactions. As we continue to navigate the digital landscape, these skills become indispensable in fostering successful and respectful communication across all platforms.

6.2 Managing Your Social Media Presence

Navigating the complex landscape of social media requires more than just understanding how to post or tweet; it demands a strategic approach to crafting an image that resonates with personal and professional circles. Social media offers a unique platform where the lines between individual expression and professional branding often blur, making it crucial to curate a presence that reflects your values and enhances your professional reputation. When constructing a digital persona suitable for potential employers or clients, start by auditing your social media profiles. Scrutinize each post, image, and shared link to ensure they align with the professional image you aim to project. This might mean pruning photos that don't fit the professional mold or tweaking your bio to highlight skills and experiences relevant to your career goals.

As the digital realm becomes increasingly integrated into daily life, maintaining strict privacy settings is not just advisable; it's imperative. Each social media platform has tools and options designed to help you control who sees your posts, interacts with your content, and accesses your personal information. Please familiarize yourself with these settings and adjust them to suit your comfort level and professional needs. For instance, platforms like Facebook allow you to customize the visibility of each post. Utilize these features to create layers of accessibility, perhaps keeping more casual posts limited to close friends while sharing professional achievements more broadly. Moreover, updating your privacy settings is essential as platforms often change their policies and features.

Engagement on social media shouldn't be sporadic or purely reactionary; it should be a consistent and thoughtful process. Effective engagement means posting regularly and interacting in a way that strengthens your professional image. This includes sharing relevant articles, commenting on industry news, and participating in discussions that underscore your expertise and interests. Such interactions demonstrate your active involvement in your field and help build a network of colleagues and thought leaders who recognize your contributions. The frequency of your posts plays a role, too— too much can overwhelm your audience, while too little can make you seem disengaged. Finding that sweet spot is critical, ensuring your presence is consistent but not overpowering.

Handling negative interactions online can be particularly challenging, but handling them professionally and poise is crucial for maintaining your reputation. When you encounter negative comments or messages, take a moment to assess the best course of action. If a comment is constructive criticism, acknowledging the feedback and responding thoughtfully can turn a potentially harmful interaction into a demonstration of your professionalism and ability to engage in productive dialogue. However, if the comments are derogatory or inflammatory, it may be more prudent to ignore them or, if necessary, block the user and report the behavior to the platform. Deciding when to respond and when to step back is a delicate balance and should be guided by the potential impact on your professional image and emotional well-being.

In managing your social media presence, remember that each post, like, and comment contributes to a broader narrative about who you are and what you represent. By carefully curating content, maintaining stringent privacy controls, engaging thoughtfully, and handling negativity tactfully, you can leverage social media as a powerful tool to shape and showcase a professional image that opens doors to opportunities and establishes you as a respected voice in your industry. As we continue to explore the nuances of digital communication, remember that each platform offers unique tools and opportunities to enhance your professional journey, making it essential to adapt and refine your strategies to stay relevant and impactful in the ever-evolving digital landscape.

6.3 Video Calls: Presenting Your Best Self Online

In the digital era, video calls have become a cornerstone of professional and personal communication. Whether it's a team meeting, a job interview, or a catch-up with friends, presenting yourself well in a video call is invaluable. The first step to ensuring a professional appearance on video calls is setting up the right technical environment. This begins with choosing the correct equipment. While most laptops and smartphones have built-in cameras and microphones, investing in a high-quality external webcam and microphone can significantly enhance audio-visual clarity. Position your camera at eye level to simulate direct eye contact with your conversation partners, mimicking the face-to-face interaction dynamic. Lighting also plays a pivotal role; soft, natural light sources in front of you can illuminate your face clearly, avoiding shadows and overexposure, which could distract from the interaction.

Moreover, be mindful of your background. A cluttered or distracting backdrop can divert attention away from the conversation. Opt for a neutral background or one professionally set up with minimal distractions, perhaps a bookshelf with a few curated items or a clean, plain wall.

Once your technical setup is optimized, focusing on your on-camera presence is the next critical step. Maintaining eye contact with the camera rather than looking at the screen can create a sense of engagement and directness often lost in digital communication. Your body language also significantly impacts how you are perceived. Sit upright and lean slightly forward to show attentiveness. Gestures can effectively emphasize points but should be used sparingly and within the camera's frame to avoid looking exaggerated. Active listening cues such as nodding and verbal affirmatives like "I under-stand" or "That makes sense" can also help demonstrate engagement and encourage further dialogue. These subtle cues reassure the speaker that you are fully present and invested in the conversation, fostering a more effective and meaningful exchange.

Managing distractions is equally crucial to maintaining profes-sionalism during video calls. Distractions can range from back-ground noise to pop-up notifications on your screen. Before your call, ensure your environment is as controlled as possible—inform others in your space that you will be on a call to avoid interruptions, close doors to minimize noise, and use headphones with a microphone to isolate audio input and output. On the technical side, turning off notifications on your computer and phone can prevent pop-ups from diverting your attention and disrupting the flow of conversation. If an interruption occurs, handling it gracefully is key; apologize briefly, address the disruption quickly, and refocus on the call. This shows that you respect the time and attention of all participants.

Preparation is crucial for successful communication, and video calls are no exception. Treat these digital interactions with the same seriousness as in-person meetings. This means punctuality, dressing appropriately, and coming prepared with all necessary documents and points you wish to discuss. Additionally, just as you would follow up a face-to-face meeting with a summary email or a thank-you note, doing the same after a video call can reinforce the importance of the discussion and provide a record of what was agreed upon. This follow-up demonstrates professionalism and helps keep projects and relationships moving forward by ensuring all participants are aligned and aware of the next steps.

By meticulously setting up your technology, mastering your on-camera presence, managing potential distractions, and preparing thoroughly for every encounter, you ensure that your video calls reflect your professionalism and dedication, regardless of the physical distance. These practices enhance your effectiveness in video communications and strengthen your relationships, paving the way for more productive and engaging interactions in our increasingly digital world.

6.4 The Etiquette of Online Messaging and Emails

In the digital realm, where conversations flow continuously across various platforms, the clarity and conciseness of your messages are paramount. Every email or message serves as a building block in your professional relationships and personal connections. Therefore, ensuring each communication is clear and concise is crucial to avoid the pitfalls of misinterpretation that can lead to unnecessary complications. When you write an email or a message, think of it as a mini-presentation of your thoughts and intentions. Start by stating the purpose of your communication early in the text to set the right expectations. Follow this by providing the necessary details that support your initial statement. This structure helps the recipient quickly grasp the essence of your message without wading through unnecessary verbosity. It's about respecting the recipient's time and cognitive load—ensuring they can understand your message without effort. Avoid using ambiguous terms or complex jargon that might confuse the reader. Instead, opt for simple language and short sentences that effectively convey your points. This practice improves the readability of your messages and enhances the overall communication flow, making your interactions more productive and enjoyable.

Adhering to professional standards in your digital communications reflects your respect for yourself and your correspondent. This starts with how you format your emails. Use a professional font and size, ensure your text is aligned, and keep your formatting clean and consistent. How you open and close your emails also plays a critical role in setting the tone of your interaction. Traditional salutations like "Dear" followed by the recipient's name or title show formality and respect, particularly in initial communications or formal exchanges. Concluding your emails with phrases like "Best regards" or "Sincerely" followed by your name adds a touch of professionalism and provides a clear end to your message. These seemingly small elements contribute significantly to the perception of your professional identity and can influence the dynamics of your professional relationships.

Timing your messages can be as crucial as the content itself. Understanding when to send business emails and messages is critical to ensuring they receive the attention they deserve. This includes being mindful of different time zones when dealing with international colleagues or clients. For instance, sending an email late in the evening might be convenient for you but could be the start of a busy workday for someone on the other side of the globe, and as such, your email might get lost in the morning influx. A good practice is to schedule your emails to be sent during the recipient's local business hours. This increases the likelihood of your email being read promptly and shows consideration for the recipient's work schedule and commitments. Additionally, understanding the workweek's flow can help time your communications effectively. For example, Monday mornings are often busy with catch-ups and planning, making it less ideal for sending non-urgent communications, which might be better-received mid-week.

Handling sensitive or complex topics via digital communications often requires a nuanced approach. While emails and online messages offer convenience, they lack the tone and context that face-to-face or telephonic conversations can provide. This can lead to misinterpretations, especially when discussing nuanced or emotionally charged topics. In such cases, it's advisable to use digital communications to set the stage for a conversation—perhaps outlining the topic and suggesting a meeting or call to discuss it in detail. This approach allows you to address complex issues with the clarity and depth they require, fostering better understanding and decision-making. For instance, an email can schedule a meeting if you need to discuss a performance issue with a team member. At the same time, the conversation can take place in a more personal setting where tone and body language can help convey empathy and constructiveness, which are often not translatable in written form. This strategy ensures that sensitive topics are handled with the care they deserve and preserves the integrity and effectiveness of your communications.

6.5 Balancing Digital and Face-to-Face Communication

In an era where digital conversations often overshadow face-to-face interactions, choosing the suitable medium for your message is more crucial than ever. This decision can significantly influence the effectiveness of your communication, affecting everything from the clarity of your message to the depth of your relationships. When deciding whether to send a quick text, shoot an email, or arrange a meeting, consider the nature of the message and the desired outcome. Complex issues, especially those that might evoke strong emotions, generally benefit from in-person discussions where nuances can be better understood and empathy more effectively conveyed. Conversely, straightforward updates or scheduling confirmations can be efficiently handled through digital mediums, saving time and resources.

Integrating digital tools into personal interactions has transformed how we organize and maintain our social lives. Apps and digital platforms offer unprecedented convenience for managing group activities, from family gatherings to more significant events. Tools like shared calendars help synchronize schedules, while event planning apps can streamline everything from invitations to menu planning and logistical arrangements. These tools not only facilitate the mechanics of organizing but also enhance the experience of connecting, allowing more time to be spent enjoying the company of others rather than managing the details.

Maintaining personal connections in today's mobile and often transient world can be challenging, mainly when physical presence is limited. Digital communication offers a lifeline in these situations, allowing for regular check-ins and updates that keep relationships vibrant. Utilizing a mix of communication forms—from messaging and video calls to sharing photos and social media interactions—can help keep a sense of closeness despite physical distances. Keeping these interactions regular but unforced is essential, ensuring they are a natural part of your relationship dynamics. For instance, a weekly video call can become a cherished ritual that all parties look forward to, providing a consistent opportunity to connect face-to-face, even if through a screen.

Transitioning between digital and face-to-face communication can sometimes feel jarring, but it can be seamless with thoughtful planning. Preparing for in-person meetings with the same rigor as online interactions is critical. For meetings originating from digital conversations, ensure continuity by reviewing previous correspondences and bringing any necessary documents to the meeting. This preparation shows respect and attentiveness, which strengthens professional and personal bonds. Similarly, after a face-to-face meeting, following up with a digital message reinforces the points discussed and demonstrates your engagement and commitment to the relationship or project.

Navigating when and how to use digital and face-to-face communication effectively is essential in our interconnected world. By understanding the strengths and limitations of each medium and using them to complement each other, you can enhance your personal and professional interactions, ensuring that your communications are heard and felt. As we wrap up this chapter on digital communication strategies, remember that the goal is not just to keep up with the pace of technology but to use it to forge deeper, more meaningful connections that enrich our lives and the lives of those around us.

In the next chapter, we will explore the personal development opportunities that arise from mastering these communication skills, setting the stage for continued growth and success in all areas of life.

7

PERSONAL DEVELOPMENT THROUGH COMMUNICATION

Imagine stepping into a room where every voice, including yours, resonates with clarity and purpose. Communication is not just about exchanging information; it's about understanding and enhancing your voice amidst the chorus. Personal development through communication begins with a deep understanding of your communication style. This journey of self-discovery sharpens your interaction skills and mirrors your personal growth as you navigate various life scenarios.

7.1 Self-Awareness: Understanding Your Communication Style

At the heart of effective communication lies an understanding of oneself. Recognizing your unique communication style is akin to finding your voice in a crowded room. This self-awareness is critical as it influences how you convey thoughts, respond to others, and navigate social interactions. To begin this exploration, consider engaging with various self-assessment tools to reveal aspects of your communication style. These tools often categorize communication behaviors into types or styles, such as assertive, passive, aggressive, or passive-aggressive, each with distinct characteristics.

Reflecting on past interactions provides valuable insights into your communication habits. Think back to a recent discussion that went exceptionally well and one that did not. Analyze what you said, how you said it, and your body language. Did your style facilitate understanding and cooperation, or did it lead to confusion or conflict? Understanding these dynamics is crucial in identifying your communication style's strengths and weaknesses. For instance, you might discover a tendency to dominate conversations, which can be seen as assertive in some contexts but aggressive in others.

Once you have a clearer picture of your communication tendencies, the next step is to learn how to adapt your style to different situations effectively. This flexibility significantly enhances your interactions and relationships. If your style is predominantly passive, you might find yourself frequently overlooked in discussions. Practicing assertiveness, such as voicing your opinions clearly and respectfully, can alter how you are perceived and treated. Conversely, if you tend to be overly assertive, tempering your approach and listening more can foster better collaboration and reduce conflicts.

Real-Life Application

To solidify your understanding of your communication style and its impact, I encourage you to experiment with adjusting it in safe environments. This could be in a casual conversation with a friend or a less critical meeting at work. After these interactions, reflect on the changes you made, how they affected the dynamics of the conversation, and how they made you feel. Were you more effective in getting your point across? Did people respond more positively? This ongoing practice builds your confidence and deepens your understanding of how to use communication for personal and professional growth.

Incorporating these strategies into your daily life isn't just about becoming a better communicator. It's about becoming a more engaged listener, thoughtful speaker, and empathetic friend and colleague. As you continue to explore and refine your communication style, you'll find that your ability to connect with others and navigate the complexities of human relationships will flourish.

7.2 Emotional Intelligence: The Key to Empathetic Communication

At its essence, emotional intelligence (EI) is the ability to perceive, control, and evaluate emotions—both your own and those of others. This skill is indispensable in effective communication as it underpins navigating interpersonal relationships judiciously and empathetically. Emotional intelligence allows you to read the room, understand the underlying sentiments behind the words, and respond in a way that fosters open and trustful dialogue. It's a cornerstone of effective leadership, conflict resolution, and, more broadly, any situation where communicating effectively is crucial to outcomes.

Understanding and managing your own emotions is the first step towards emotional intelligence. It's about knowing how your feelings affect your thoughts and actions and how others might perceive them. For instance, recognizing that stress or frustration can make your tone harsher or your comments more abrupt can help you take steps to mitigate these effects before they impact a conversation negatively. Deep breathing, taking a short walk, or pausing to collect your thoughts can help manage emotional responses. This self-regulation ensures that your communications are more considered and less reactive, which can lead to more productive interactions.

Identifying and understanding the emotions of others is equally important. This ability allows you to empathize with their perspective, crucial in building rapport and trust. It involves more than just listening to what is being said; it's also about picking up on non-verbal cues such as body language, tone of voice, and facial expressions. For example, if someone crosses their arms and avoids eye contact while saying they're open to feedback, their body language suggests they might feel defensive. Recognizing these cues enables you to adjust your approach by softening your tone or framing your feedback in a more positive and supportive manner.

Empathy in Practice

To enhance your empathy, try engaging in exercises encouraging you to consider other people's feelings and perspectives. One effective technique is the 'role reversal' exercise, where you consciously adopt someone else's viewpoint in a recent interaction. Think about their motivations, concerns, and emotional state, and consider how this might have influenced their behavior and responses. This exercise can be particularly enlightening in understanding conflicts or misunderstandings, as it helps you see the situation from the other person's perspective, often revealing insights that weren't apparent from your viewpoint.

Another practical exercise involves more direct engagement with your emotional intelligence skills. The next time you are in a meeting or a group setting, practice identifying and naming the emotions you observe in others. Afterward, reflect on how recognizing these emotions might change how you respond in future interactions. This ongoing practice improves your ability to read others and makes your responses more empathetic and practical.

Integrating emotional intelligence into your communication practices enhances personal interactions and sets a foundation for more robust, resilient relationships. Whether in personal relationships, professional settings, or casual encounters, connecting with others on an emotional level is invaluable. It enriches your interactions, making them more meaningful and productive, and ultimately, it plays a crucial role in your overall success and satisfaction in various facets of life.

7.3 Receiving and Giving Feedback Constructively

Whether given in a boardroom or over coffee, feedback is one of the most potent tools for personal and professional development. It's a bridge that connects individual effort with collective expectations and is pivotal in sharpening skills, refining projects, and enhancing relationships. The constructive exchange of feedback can transform routine tasks into opportunities for growth and innovation. However, its potential is realized only when giving and receiving feedback are approached with care and intention.

When feedback is directed towards you, receiving it gracefully is crucial. This starts with embracing an open mindset, which allows you to consider the input without immediate bias or defense. Active listening plays a vital role here. It involves more than just hearing words; it's about engaging fully with the speaker, showing genuine interest in their observations, and striving to understand their perspective. When feedback is delivered, focus solely on understanding the message, avoiding the urge to formulate a quick response. This attentiveness can be signaled through non-verbal cues such as nodding or maintaining eye contact and verbally through affirmations like "I see" or "Please go on." Once the initial message is conveyed, diving deeper through clarifying questions can unearth valuable insights and demonstrate your commitment to improvement. Questions could include, "Can you give me an example of when I did this?" or "What might be a better approach next time?" These inquiries clarify the feedback and engage the giver, making the session interactive and constructive.

Responding appropriately to feedback is the final step in the reception process. This doesn't necessarily mean agreeing with everything said but acknowledging the value of the insights provided. A simple expression of gratitude can affirm your appreciation, regardless of the nature of the feedback. If specific points require change or adjustment, outline how you plan to address them. This shows you are open to feedback and proactive about utilizing it for personal growth.

On the flip side, giving feedback is an art that requires meticulous care to ensure it is both heard and heeded. The Situation-Behavior-Impact (SBI) model is a reliable framework, focusing on concrete instances rather than vague generalizations. Begin by clearly describing the situation where the observed behavior occurred. This sets the context and ensures both parties think about the same event. Next, detail the specific behavior without infusing personal judgment. For example, instead of saying, "You were disruptive," try, "During the meeting when you interrupted others while they were speaking..." This precision prevents the recipient from feeling unjustly criticized and focuses the discussion on observable facts. Lastly, describe the impact of this behavior on you or the team. For instance, "This made it difficult for others to share their ideas, which we needed to hear." Highlighting the impact helps the receiver see the consequences of their actions and underscores the need for change.

Creating a Feedback Culture

Fostering an environment where feedback is routinely given and received can significantly enhance a team or organization's dynamics. It starts with leadership; when leaders actively solicit and handle input constructively, they set a powerful example for others. Integrating regular feedback sessions into the routine, such as during project debriefs or one-on-one meetings, normalizes the practice. Establishing clear guidelines for giving and receiving feedback is also beneficial, as it can alleviate anxiety and prevent miscommunication.

Encouraging a feedback-rich culture is not merely about pointing out areas for improvement; it is equally important to acknowledge and celebrate what works well. Positive feedback can boost morale and motivate individuals to maintain and elevate their performance when given genuinely and frequently. It reinforces good practices and behaviors, making them more likely to be repeated, and shows that feedback is not just about criticism but about building on existing strengths.

Through these strategies, feedback becomes less about evaluation and more about insightful dialogue that propels individuals and groups toward higher levels of achievement and fulfillment. As you engage with feedback actively, remember its dual role as a mirror reflecting your current state and a map guiding your ongoing development.

7.4 The Role of Mindfulness in Communication

Mindfulness, often seen as a practice reserved for meditation or yoga, enhances communication. At its core, mindfulness involves maintaining a moment-by-moment awareness of our thoughts, feelings, bodily sensations, and surrounding environment. This heightened awareness can transform how you interact with others, making your communication more intentional, focused, and effective. Being fully present allows you to listen and respond more thoughtfully, fostering deeper connections and reducing misunderstandings.

Mindful Listening

One essential application of mindfulness in communication is mindful listening. This practice requires you to focus entirely on the speaker, absorbing not just the words but the message conveyed. This means setting aside your thoughts and judgments while listening, allowing you to truly hear what is being said without the distraction of formulating a response. To practice mindful listening, start by centering yourself before a conversation begins. Take a deep breath and commit to being fully present. Concentrate on their words, tone, and body language as the other person speaks. Notice any emotional reactions these evoke in you, but let them pass without judgment. If you find your mind wandering, gently bring your focus back to the speaker. This attentive listening can significantly enhance your understanding and appreciation of the conversation, leading to more meaningful interactions.

Mindful listening is not just about hearing words; it's about connecting with the speaker on a deeper level. It involves empathy and a genuine curiosity about what they are expressing. This can be particularly effective when emotions run high or the stakes are significant. By giving your full attention, you signal to the speaker that they are valued and that their thoughts and feelings matter. This can help de-escalate conflicts and build stronger, more respectful personal and professional relationships.

Mindful Speaking

Conversely, mindful speaking involves being acutely aware of your communication. This includes paying attention to the words you choose, the tone of your voice, and how others might receive your message. Before you speak, take a moment to consider your intentions and the impact your words could have. Ask yourself if what you are about to say is accurate, necessary, and kind. This brief pause can distinguish between a reactive response that might escalate tensions and a thoughtful reply that contributes positively to the dialogue.

Being aware of your nonverbal communication is also essential when practicing mindful speaking. Your facial expressions, gestures, and posture all convey messages that can support or contradict what you are saying. Awareness of these nonverbal cues ensures that your entire message—both spoken and unspoken—is coherent and clear. This consistency helps prevent misunderstandings and strengthens your credibility and authenticity.

Incorporating Mindfulness Practices

Integrating mindfulness into your daily communication practices can be a manageable change to your routine. Simple, intentional actions can make a significant difference. For example, before an important meeting or conversation, take a few minutes to practice a brief mindfulness exercise. This could be a short meditation focusing on your breath or a few moments spent quietly gathering your thoughts. This preparation helps you enter the conversation with a clear, focused mind, ready to engage fully.

Another practical way to incorporate mindfulness is to establish regular check-ins with yourself throughout the day. These can be brief pauses where you assess your current state of mind and adjust as needed. For instance, if you find yourself feeling rushed or distracted, a quick mindfulness break can help reset your focus. During these pauses, practice observing your thoughts and feelings without judgment, allowing them to pass through your mind like clouds drifting across the sky. This can help reduce stress and increase calmness, improving communication.

By embracing mindfulness in your communication practices, you enhance your interactions with others and contribute to a greater sense of well-being in your own life. Whether through mindful listening, speaking, or the intentional integration of mindfulness exercises, these practices foster a deeper connection to the present moment and enrich your relationships with greater empathy and understanding.

7.5 Continuous Learning and Adaptation in Communication Skills

Embracing a mindset of lifelong learning in communication is not merely beneficial; it's essential for personal and professional growth. Communication is a dynamic skill set influenced by evolving social norms, technological advancements, and cultural shifts. Understanding that your development as an effective communicator is never complete can transform how you interact with the world, making you more adaptable, thoughtful, and impactful in your conversations. This approach requires an ongoing commitment to learning and self-improvement, recognizing that each conversation is an opportunity to learn something new about yourself, others, and the art of communication itself.

As society evolves, so too do the norms and expectations around communication. What was appropriate a decade ago may now be passé or even offensive today. Attention to these shifts is crucial, particularly in multicultural and multi-generational settings. For instance, the rapid digitalization of communication has introduced new norms around responsiveness and privacy, challenging traditional perceptions of communication in professional settings. Similarly, cultural diversity within workplaces and social spaces demands an awareness and respect for different communication styles and practices. Staying informed about these changes requires an active engagement with diverse groups and a willingness to listen and learn from experiences different from your own. It also involves keeping up with academic and industry-specific literature that addresses contemporary communication challenges and strategies.

To support your continuous learning, a wealth of resources is available that can deepen your understanding and enhance your skills. Books on communication cover a broad range of topics, from interpersonal dynamics to public speaking and digital etiquette.

Workshops and seminars offer more interactive opportunities for learning, often providing scenarios that simulate real-life communication challenges. These settings allow you to learn from experts and offer the chance to receive immediate feedback on your communication strategies. Podcasts and online courses are increasingly popular platforms for exploring communication topics at your own pace and can be particularly useful for delving into niche subjects that interest you. For instance, podcasts focusing on emotional intelligence or cross-cultural communication provide insights and tips that can be directly applied to your daily interactions.

Creating personal feedback loops is another powerful strategy for ongoing development. This involves regularly assessing your communication experiences and outcomes, setting specific goals for improvement, and adjusting your plan based on feedback. Start by keeping a communication journal where you note fundamental interactions, observations about what went well and what didn't, and any insights you gained. Review this journal periodically to identify patterns or recurring challenges. Set goals based on these insights, such as working on your active listening skills or improving your ability to handle conflict. Seek feedback from trusted colleagues, friends, or mentors who can honestly assess your communication style and progress. This feedback is invaluable as it provides an external perspective on your effectiveness and impact.

Committing to a lifelong learning approach to communication ensures that your skills remain relevant and sharp, no matter how the norms and mediums evolve. This continuous adaptation enhances your interactions and positions you as a competent and considerate communicator in professional settings. As you integrate these practices into your life, you'll find that your ability to connect with others deepens, and your personal and professional relationships become more fulfilling and productive.

As this chapter concludes, remember that the journey to becoming an effective communicator is continuous. Each step you take to learn more about how communication works and how you can improve your skills contributes to a broader understanding of yourself and the world around you. These efforts enhance immediate interactions and enrich your longer-term relationships and career prospects. In the next chapter, we will explore navigating social dynamics, where these communication skills will be applied to deepen bonds and understand the complexities of interacting in various social settings.

8

———————

NAVIGATING SOCIAL DYNAMICS

Imagine stepping into a bustling coffee shop where every table tells a different story. Every group interaction unfolds with its unique dynamics. Some tables radiate laughter and ease, while others are calm and dotted with thoughtful nods and intense gazes. This scene is a microcosm of the complex social dynamics that permeate every aspect of our lives—from casual meet-ups to formal gatherings. Understanding the underlying forces in these interactions can significantly enhance your ability to navigate and influence social environments. In this chapter, we dive deep into the fabric of group dynamics, exploring how roles, norms, and cohesiveness shape collective behaviors and how mastering these elements can transform your social interactions.

8.1 Understanding Group Dynamics in Social Settings

Basics of Group Dynamics

At the core of group dynamics lies the understanding that groups are more than just the sum of their parts. They are complex systems influenced by various factors that govern how members interact. Firstly, roles within a group often define the behavior of its members.

These roles can be formal, like a designated leader or secretary, or informal, like a peacemaker or the group's leading provocateur. Each role has expectations that can significantly influence how individuals behave, and others perceive them.

Norms are the shared expectations and rules that guide behavior in a group. They can be explicit, like written codes of conduct, or implicit, understood through day-to-day interactions. Norms dictate everything from how members communicate to how they dress and respond to conflict. Cohesiveness, or the extent to which members feel bonded and united, impacts a group's stability, performance, and satisfaction. High cohesiveness often enhances group productivity and emotional security but can also lead to groupthink, where the desire for harmony results in poor decision-making processes.

Observing Group Interactions

To truly understand the dynamics of a group, one must become a keen observer. Watching how group members interact can provide insights into the roles and norms that govern their behavior. Pay attention to who speaks, who listens, and how decisions are made. Notice non-verbal cues like body language and eye contact, which can reveal more about the group's true sentiments than their words might suggest. This observational practice can be particularly enlightening in new settings where you're trying to gauge a group's cultural and social fabric before engaging fully.

Adapting to Different Groups

Once you grasp a group's dynamics, adapting your communication style to fit can significantly enhance your integration and effectiveness within the group. If a group values directness, tempering your circumspect communication style can improve your acceptance and influence. Conversely, in a group that prizes consensus, fostering open dialogue and showing appreciation for diverse opinions can make you a valued member. Adaptation doesn't mean losing your individuality; it's about finding how your unique attributes can contribute to the group's existing framework.

Conflict Resolution in Groups

Conflicts are inevitable in any group setting, but their management determines the health and progress of group interactions. Effective conflict resolution involves understanding the underlying causes of conflict, which often relate to unmet needs or clashing values. Mediation techniques can be pivotal here. They focus on facilitating dialogue between conflicting parties to find a mutually acceptable solution. Encouraging open communication, where members feel safe to express dissenting opinions without fear of reprisal, can prevent many conflicts from escalating. Moreover, fostering a collaborative environment, where conflict is seen as a catalyst for growth rather than a disruptor, can transform how group members interact during challenging times.

Interactive Element: Group Role Identification Exercise

To enhance your understanding of group dynamics, engage in this exercise during your next group interaction. Take a piece of paper and list all the members of the group. Next to each name, write down the role you perceive they play within the group (e.g., leader, challenger, supporter). Reflect on how these roles influence the group's interactions and your behavior within the group. This exercise will improve your observational skills and help you see the impact of roles on group dynamics more clearly.

By mastering the complexities of group dynamics, you equip yourself with the tools to navigate any social setting more effectively. Understanding the subtle forces guiding group interactions is critical whether you want to enhance your influence in professional settings, foster better friendships, or lead more effectively. As you continue to apply these insights, you'll find that your ability to understand and influence social dynamics becomes a powerful tool in your interpersonal toolkit.

8.2 The Influence of Social Hierarchies on Communication

In every social interaction, whether in a boardroom or at a family gathering, a lattice of social hierarchies subtly dictates the flow of conversation and power dynamics. These hierarchies are not merely constructs of corporate or organizational settings but are prevalent in all social structures. They determine who leads the dialogue, whose ideas are prioritized, and how openly individuals can express themselves. Understanding these hierarchies is crucial because it helps you navigate complex social waters with more agility and confidence, ensuring that your voice is not just heard but also respected.

Social hierarchies are often established based on a combination of roles, seniority, expertise, and even interpersonal relationships. In formal settings like workplaces, these are delineated: managers have authority over staff, senior staff over juniors. In informal settings, though, they can be more nuanced. For instance, in a family, an elder might hold more sway in decisions, or in a group of friends, the one with the most assertive personality might dominate discussions. Recognizing these hierarchies allows you to tailor your communication to respect existing dynamics while ensuring your participation is impactful.

Navigating these hierarchical structures effectively requires observation, adaptability, and strategic communication. Start by observing how interactions unfold around you. Notice who initiates conversations, how decisions are made, and how others align their responses. This will give you a clearer picture of the underlying power dynamics. Once you understand this, you can adapt your communication style accordingly. For instance, if you're meeting with higher-ups, framing your suggestions as questions or inputs might be wiser rather than outright challenging. This approach respects authority and invites engagement without disrupting the established hierarchy.

Influencing upwards in a hierarchy demands a careful balance between assertiveness and tact. When you need to influence decision-makers or higher-status individuals, start by building a foundation of trust and respect. One effective way to do this is by consistently demonstrating competence and reliability. When you speak up, ensure your ideas are well-thought-out and backed by data or well-reasoned arguments. Presenting your thoughts in a way that aligns with the organization's goals or the leadership's interests can also increase your influence. For instance, if proposing a new project, highlight how it aligns with the company's strategic objectives or might solve a problem that a senior leader has prioritized.

Handling power dynamics gracefully is one of the most challenging aspects of navigating social hierarchies. It requires a keen sense of timing, the ability to read the room, and the emotional intelligence to understand and empathize with different perspectives. Always be respectful in your interactions and stand firm in your values and ideas. If you feel sidelined in a discussion, politely assert your desire to contribute. Phrases like, "I have some thoughts on this that I believe could add value," can signal your interest in contributing without coming across as confrontive. It's also vital to be receptive to others' viewpoints and open to compromise. This flexibility helps maintain harmony and enhances your reputation as a collaborative and thoughtful participant.

Navigating social hierarchies effectively isn't just about observing rules or muting your personality. It's about understanding the context you're operating in and using this understanding to communicate in the most effective way possible. Whether stepping into a new role, participating in a family event, or engaging in community activities, maneuvering through these social structures can significantly enhance your interactions and communications outcomes. By approaching each situation with awareness and strategic insight, you ensure that your contributions are noticed and valued, paving the way for more meaningful and impactful exchanges.

8.3 Bridging the Gap: Communicating Across Generations

In today's diverse social and professional landscapes, the ability to communicate across generations is not just a nicety—it's a necessity. Understanding each generation's distinct characteristics and preferences can significantly enhance your ability to engage effectively with various audiences. Let's start by painting a broad picture of the generational landscape.

Baby Boomers, born between 1946 and 1964, tend to value stability and are known for their strong work ethic and loyalty to their employers. Their communication preferences lean towards more formal styles, and they appreciate direct, face-to-face interactions. Generation X, born between 1965 and 1980, often called the 'latchkey' generation, values independence and adaptability. They bridge the gap between the traditionalist Boomers and the tech-savvy younger generations, comfortable with both phone calls and emails. Millennials, born between 1981 and 1996, are digital natives who value flexibility and purpose in their work. They prefer fast and digital communication, favoring texting and social media platforms. Finally, Generation Z, born from 1997 onward, values authenticity and individuality, strongly favoring visual and digital communication modes, such as videos and social media content.

Adapting your communication to meet these varied preferences involves more than choosing the right words; it involves respecting and understanding each group's underlying values and expectations. For instance, when engaging with Baby Boomers, adopting a more formal tone and focusing on building credibility and trust through face-to-face meetings or detailed phone conversations is beneficial. Combining respect for their independence with a straightforward and flexible communication style can be effective with Gen Xers. This might mean providing options for how and when to communicate, allowing them to choose what works best for them.

When communicating with Millennials and Gen Z, digital fluency is key. Utilizing concise messaging through texts or engaging visuals on social media platforms can capture their attention much more effectively than lengthy emails or printed memos. However, it's crucial to balance being informal and maintaining professionalism, as these younger generations still value insightful, respectful communication. Engaging them with interactive content, such as polls or open-ended questions on digital platforms, draws their attention and fosters a sense of participation and engagement.

The role of technology in bridging these generational gaps cannot be overstated. Each generation has its preferred platforms—from the stability and formality of email for Baby Boomers to the dynamic, instant nature of Twitter, now X, or Instagram stories favored by younger generations. Understanding which platforms will most likely reach your intended audience can significantly enhance your communication efficacy. For instance, LinkedIn can be a powerful tool for professional interactions across all generations, offering a blend of traditional business communication with modern digital engagement.

Creating messages that resonate across generations requires a focus on universal themes and inclusive language. Themes such as success, security, and community resonate widely and can be tailored to specific generational concerns with slight modifications in language and presentation. For example, while you might highlight the stability and long-term benefits of a business strategy to Baby Boomers, the same strategy might be framed as innovative and socially responsible to appeal to Millennials and Gen Z.

Inclusive language also plays a critical role in multigenerational communication. This involves avoiding jargon or cultural references that might not be familiar to all age groups and focusing instead on clear, concise, understandable language. It also means being mindful of the assumptions that can often be embedded in our words and trying to respect and validate the experiences and perspectives of each generation.

By carefully considering these aspects of generational communication, you can effectively bridge the gap between diverse age groups, enhancing both your personal interactions and professional engagements. Whether you are presenting to a mixed-age audience, marketing a new product, or simply looking to foster better relationships across age divides, these strategies provide a foundation for more precise, more effective communication that respects and values the unique contributions of each generation.

8.4 Making a Mark: Influencing Without Authority

In the labyrinth of professional and social interactions, the ability to influence without holding formal authority is akin to discovering a hidden superpower. It's about persuading and negotiating, not through the mantle of power but through the force of your ideas, relationships, and character. Understanding how to wield this power can transform your interactions across various spheres of life, from the office to community groups, allowing you to catalyze change and inspire action, irrespective of your position.

The art of influence without authority begins with the mastery of persuasion and negotiation skills. Persuasion is not about manipulation; instead, it's about presenting your ideas in ways that resonate deeply with others, aligning your visions and goals with their values and needs. Effective persuasion involves clear communication, emotional intelligence, and the strategic use of facts and emotional appeals. Meanwhile, negotiation is not just for boardroom battles; it's part of everyday interactions. Whether you're negotiating project roles or deciding on a family vacation spot, the ability to find and articulate mutually beneficial solutions is crucial. Both skills are underpinned by a deep understanding of human behavior and motivations, requiring you to be a keen observer and an empathetic communicator.

Building credibility and trust is foundational in your quest to influence without authority. Credibility comes from a track record of consistency and reliability. When people believe you deliver on your promises and maintain a consistent standard in your work and interactions, your words carry more weight. Trust, on the other hand, is earned through honesty, transparency, and empathy. It involves showing genuine care for the interests and well-being of others. Credibility and trust create a powerful platform to influence others effectively. For instance, if you are known for delivering projects efficiently and with great results, colleagues are likelier to support your initiatives and adopt your suggestions, even if you do not hold a senior managerial position.

Strategic networking extends your influence by widening your circle of impact. It's about connecting within your immediate circle and including diverse groups and individuals. Effective networking involves more than exchanging business cards or LinkedIn connections; it requires engaging meaningfully with others, offering and asking for help, sharing knowledge, and maintaining regular contact. The broader your network, the more resources and alliances you have to mobilize support for your ideas and projects. For example, if you want to develop a new community outreach program, having a network that includes local business owners, school officials, and other community leaders can be invaluable. These connections can provide support, resources, and a platform to amplify your initiatives.

Leveraging soft skills such as empathy, active listening, and emotional intelligence is crucial in influencing others without authority. These skills allow you to understand and connect with people on a deeper level, which is essential when you do not have formal power. Empathy helps you see situations from others' perspectives, fostering a deeper understanding and connection. Active listening shows that you value others' inputs and are open to incorporating their views into your vision. Emotional intelligence enables you to manage both your emotions and those of others, helping you navigate conversations with sensitivity and tact. For instance, in a team meeting, being able to sense frustration and acknowledge it can help address underlying issues, making the team feel heard and supported and, thereby, more open to your influence.

By mastering these aspects of influencing without authority, you can effectively advocate for your ideas and lead initiatives, regardless of your position in the hierarchy. This skill enhances your professional capabilities and empowers you to significantly contribute to various aspects of your life, fostering environments where collaboration and mutual respect drive collective success.

8.5 Social Events: Mingling with Confidence

Attending social events can be a delightful experience, with opportunities to meet new people and strengthen existing relationships. However, with proper preparation, these occasions can be manageable. To navigate social gatherings easily, research the attendees, if possible. This could involve checking the guest list on an event's social media page or asking the host who will be there. Knowing who you'll meet can help you mentally prepare and tailor your conversation topics. For instance, if you know you'll be meeting someone from a field you're interested in, you could brush up on recent industry trends or key developments. Setting personal objectives for the event can also provide direction and purpose. Decide how many new people you'd like to meet or what outcomes you hope to achieve, whether gathering insights on a project or expanding your professional network.

Preparing conversation starters in advance is another effective strategy. Develop a small arsenal of open-ended questions to spark dialogue and more meaningful exchanges. Questions like "What's been keeping you busy lately?" or "Have you worked on any exciting projects recently?" can elicit detailed responses and show genuine interest in the other person's activities. These preparations boost your confidence and equip you to engage more meaningfully with others at the event.

Entering and exiting conversations gracefully is a subtle art that, when mastered, can significantly enhance your social agility. When joining an ongoing discussion, approach with a smile and wait for a natural pause to introduce yourself; this shows respect for the existing interaction and makes your entry less intrusive. Contributing a relevant comment or an appreciative observation about the discussion can also smooth your way into the group. Exiting conversations tactfully is just as crucial as entering them. When you need to leave a conversation, do so politely by expressing your enjoyment of the chat and excusing yourself with a reason, such as getting a drink, greeting another acquaintance, or needing to catch up with the host. This leaves both parties feeling good about the interaction and keeps the door open for future engagements.

Building rapport quickly is crucial in making the most of social interactions. Finding common ground is one of the fastest ways to establish a connection. This could be shared interests, mutual friends, or similar experiences. Once you discover a commonality, explore it further to deepen the bond. Showing genuine interest in the other person is another critical element. This means being present in the conversation, asking thoughtful follow-up questions, and responding with related comments or experiences. Positive body language also plays a significant role in building rapport. Maintain eye contact, smile naturally, and nod to show engagement. These non-verbal cues reinforce your verbal expressions and contribute to a warmer, more connected interaction.

Handling social anxiety in social settings is a common challenge, but it can be managed with practical strategies. Before attending an event, relax and visualize a positive social experience. This mental rehearsal can calm nerves and reduce anxiety. Breathing exercises can also be helpful; taking deep, slow breaths can decrease physiological anxiety symptoms, helping you maintain composure. If you feel overwhelmed during the event, permit yourself to take a break. Step outside for some fresh air or find a quieter space to regroup. Remember, it's okay to set your own pace at social events.

Navigating social events confidently is not just about making a good impression—it's about genuine connections and enjoyable interactions. With the proper preparation and mindset, you can transform any gathering into a rewarding personal and professional growth opportunity. As you continue to apply these strategies, you'll find that your confidence in social settings grows, along with your ability to connect with others effortlessly and authentically.

As this chapter on navigating social dynamics concludes, remember that the essence of successful social interactions lies in genuine connection and mutual respect. Whether you're mingling at a casual gathering or a formal event, the skills you develop will enhance your immediate experiences and enrich your broader social and professional life. Next, we will explore cultivating personal relationships, where these communication strategies are applied to deepen bonds and understand the complexities of individual interactions in various settings.

9

CULTIVATING PERSONAL RELATIONSHIPS

Imagine walking through a dense, vibrant forest where each tree, though rooted in the same soil, has branches stretching out in unique patterns, creating an intricate canopy of connections. Similarly, our relationships form an elaborate network of interactions, each connection requiring nurturing and understanding to deepen and flourish. In this chapter, we explore the art of cultivating personal relationships beyond mere acquaintances, focusing on the impact of emotional depth, active engagement, vulnerability, and consistent communication in fostering meaningful connections.

9.1 Deepening Connections: Moving Beyond Surface-Level Interactions

In the tapestry of human relationships, the threads that bind the deepest are woven with the yarn of emotional depth. Engaging in conversations that transcend the mundane and reach into the realm of personal experiences and feelings can transform casual interactions into lasting bonds. To navigate this depth, genuinely sharing your experiences and emotions is crucial. This sharing does more than reveal your inner world; it invites others to dismantle their walls and connect with you more personally. For instance, discussing a challenging personal experience, such as a career transition or a difficult decision, can prompt others to relate to similar life events, fostering an empathetic and authentic connection.

Active engagement in conversations is pivotal to deepening connections. This engagement is not passive; it involves employing strategies like active listening, where you focus entirely on the speaker, absorbing not just the words but the emotions and intentions behind them. Reflecting emotions is another powerful strategy. By verbally acknowledging and reflecting on the feelings expressed by others, you validate their emotions, making them feel understood and appreciated. Probing questions also play a critical role in this dynamic. Asking questions that delve deeper into the subjects discussed shows a genuine interest in understanding the other person. These questions might include inquiries about how specific experiences made them feel or what lessons they learned from particular events, prompting a deeper exploration of their thoughts and emotions.

Often perceived as a risk, vulnerability can be a surprising strength in building deeper connections. Allowing yourself to be vulnerable by sharing fears, hopes, and dreams can be daunting, yet it paves the way for a level of intimacy that superficial interactions lack. This openness invites others to share their vulnerabilities, creating a mutual trust that is both rare and valuable. However, navigating vulnerability with care is essential, ensuring it's appropriate to the trust built within the relationship. Gradually opening up and observing others' reactions helps gauge the degree of vulnerability the relationship can sustain at its current stage.

Consistency and patience are the soil and water that nourish the seeds of deep connections. Developing meaningful relationships requires time and consistent effort. Regular interactions, whether through face-to-face meetings, phone calls, or digital messages, keep the relationship alive and evolving. Patience is equally crucial, as trust and intimacy take time to develop. Rushing this process can overwhelm the other person and potentially stifle the natural growth of the relationship. Instead, allow each interaction to build on the last, gradually increasing the depth and breadth of your shared experiences and discussions.

Interactive Element: Journaling for Emotional Depth

Consider maintaining a reflective journal to enhance your ability to explore emotional depths in conversations. After each significant interaction, take a moment to jot down the vital emotional points discussed, how you felt during the conversation, and any new insights about the other person that came to light. This practice improves your emotional awareness and helps you track the development of your relationships, providing a clearer picture of how they are deepening over time.

9.2 Communicating in Romantic Relationships

Trust is the cornerstone of a solid and enduring connection in romantic relationships. Establishing and nurturing this trust hinges significantly on how effectively you communicate with your partner. Transparent communication involves sharing thoughts, feelings, and intentions without hidden agendas. While sometimes challenging, honesty reinforces this transparency, showing your partner they can rely on your words and actions. To cultivate trust, it's crucial to demonstrate reliability and integrity consistently; for instance, following through on promises and being open about your feelings and concerns. Regular, honest discussions about your thoughts and experiences also help maintain and deepen this trust. Such openness fosters a secure attachment and diminishes misunderstandings that could erode trust.

Conflict resolution in romantic relationships often tests the strength and resilience of the bond. Handling disagreements constructively is essential for the health of the relationship. Begin by expressing your feelings clearly and respectfully, using "I" statements to own your emotions and avoid blaming your partner. For example, instead of saying, "You make me feel ignored," you might say, "I feel lonely when we don't spend much time together." This approach helps keep the discussion centered on your feelings and needs without making your partner feel attacked. Listening plays a crucial role here; it involves more than hearing words. It requires empathy, understanding the emotions behind the words, and validating those feelings. This empathetic listening can transform a potential argument into a constructive discussion, paving the way for mutual understanding and solutions.

Expressing needs and desires clearly and respectfully is another pillar of healthy romantic communication. It's crucial to articulate your needs without fear or hesitation. This clarity prevents resentment that can build up when needs are not met simply because they were never clearly expressed. Start these conversations with affirmations of what works well in the relationship, then lead into your needs or desires. For example, you might say, "I appreciate your support after my long workdays. I also need some quiet time each night to unwind by myself." This method, known as "positive sandwiching," wraps potentially sensitive requests with positive statements, making it easier for your partner to receive and respond to your needs. Mutual understanding and support are nurtured when partners recognize and value their needs.

Maintaining intimacy and connection in a relationship requires dedicated effort and time. In the hustle of daily life, it's easy for couples to drift into routines prioritizing efficiency over emotional connection. Setting aside regular times to nurture your relationship is beneficial to counter this. This could be a weekly date night, a daily uninterrupted conversation, or weekend getaways. During these times, focus entirely on each other by sharing thoughts, feelings, and experiences or engaging in activities that both of you enjoy. This dedicated time strengthens emotional bonds and rekindles intimacy, reminding both partners of the joy and love that brought them together—moreover, engaging in shared activities, whether a cooking class, hiking, or attending a music event, can create shared experiences that enhance companionship and deepen your bond.

In romantic relationships, the intertwining of trust, honest communication, mutual support, and shared joy forms the blueprint for a lasting and loving partnership. By prioritizing these elements, you lay a solid foundation to support the relationship through life's myriad challenges and phases. As you and your partner continue to grow and evolve, these practices provide the flexibility and strength to adapt and flourish together.

9.3 Family Dynamics: Improving Communication at Home

Navigating the intricate dance of family dynamics involves understanding each member's roles. In many families, these roles are as varied as they are vital. There's the caretaker who ensures everyone's needs are met, the peacemaker who smooths over conflicts, or the organizer who keeps the family's schedule running smoothly. Recognizing these roles can significantly improve communication by helping you tailor your interactions to fit each person's expected contributions and perspectives. For instance, when you understand that your older sibling thrives in the organizer role, you might consult them about logistical matters rather than emotional ones, which they might find more challenging. Similarly, acknowledging the emotional support often provided by a family member in the caretaker role can lead to more effective, empathetic communication during times of stress, avoiding misunderstandings that can arise from mismatched expectations and communication styles.

The mosaic of communication styles within a family can range from those who prefer direct, concise dialogue to those who express themselves best through stories and elaborate explanations. Understanding and respecting these differences is crucial. For example, a family member who communicates straightforwardly might find long anecdotes frustrating, while another might see them as a rich, engaging way to share insights and experiences. These styles can be bridged by fostering an environment where each person's communication style is acknowledged and valued. This involves actively encouraging family members to express their thoughts in ways that reflect their natural styles while teaching them to adapt to others' preferences. For instance, during family discussions, you could encourage a balance by asking direct questions to those who prefer concise communication and inviting storytellers to elaborate on topics where more depth and detail would be beneficial.

Handling conflicts within family settings often requires a deft touch, balancing respect for individual feelings with the need to maintain harmony. Effective conflict resolution strategies include establishing clear guidelines for respectful communication, such as avoiding personal attacks and focusing on the present issue. Mediating family disputes often involves encouraging members to express their feelings and perspectives openly, ensuring everyone feels heard and validated. This can be facilitated through family meetings where each person is given the floor to speak uninterrupted, using "I" statements to express their feelings without casting blame. For example, saying, "I feel overlooked when decisions are made without my input" instead of "You never listen to me" can help reduce defensiveness and open the door to more constructive dialogue. Creating a cooperative atmosphere, where the family views conflicts as shared problems to be solved together rather than battles to be won, can transform potentially divisive situations into opportunities for strengthening family bonds.

Building a supportive and open communication environment within the family requires intentional efforts to foster inclusivity and openness. Regular family meetings can serve as a structured way to ensure everyone stays connected and informed about each other's lives, providing a regular forum for discussing issues, planning family activities, and making decisions collectively. These meetings can be supplemented by establishing shared family goals and values, which provide a common direction and purpose, reinforcing the family's identity and cohesion. Engaging in shared activities, such as regular outings, holiday traditions, or family projects, also strengthens the familial bond, creating shared experiences and memories that can serve as a foundation for deeper relationships. By actively creating an environment where open communication, mutual respect, and shared experiences are prioritized, families can build a dynamic where each member feels valued and supported, paving the way for more meaningful and satisfying family relationships.

9.4 Friendships: Maintaining Old and Building New Ones

Navigating the ever-evolving landscape of friendships requires a dedication to preserving long-standing relationships and welcoming new connections. Maintaining old friendships often hinges on consistent communication, reliability, and a heartfelt appreciation of each other's company. It's easy to let these relationships drift in our busy lives, but setting reminders to catch up, whether through a quick text or a scheduled call, can keep the bond alive. Reliability, or being there when you promise, cements trust and shows your friends they are a priority. Celebrating their successes, acknowledging their challenges, and remembering important dates like birthdays or milestones enrich your connections, making them more robust and resilient.

While nurturing old friendships is essential, branching out and forming new ones can inject fresh perspectives and energy into your life. Being open to new experiences is crucial in this process. This might mean saying yes to invitations that take you outside your comfort zone or exploring new hobbies and activities that broaden your social circle. Joining groups or clubs that align with your interests provides a natural setting for meeting people who share your passions, facilitating more accessible and meaningful conversations. Initiating conversations might feel daunting, but a simple introduction or comment about a shared situation can often break the ice. Following up after your initial meeting by suggesting another hangout or sending a message about a topic you discussed can show your interest in deepening the connection and laying the groundwork for a new friendship.

Balancing multiple social circles is akin to juggling: it requires awareness, timing, and giving each connection its due without overextending yourself. It's helpful to occasionally assess your social commitments to ensure they align with your current priorities and energy levels. Using digital tools like calendars can help you manage your time efficiently, ensuring you maintain regular contact with each circle. It's also important to be transparent with your friends about your availability and proactive in scheduling time together, which shows that you value and respect your shared time. This balance helps prevent feelings of neglect and enriches your social life with a diverse range of relationships and experiences.

Changes in friendships are inevitable due to geographical moves, evolving interests, or new life stages such as marriage or parenthood. These transitions can strain relationships, but you can adapt and maintain these bonds with thoughtful communication and flexibility. When friends move away, leveraging technology to stay connected through video calls, social media, or messaging apps can help bridge the physical distance. Sharing regular updates and making efforts to visit each other can keep the friendship vibrant. If interests begin to diverge, finding new common ground or showing interest in each other's new hobbies can provide fresh avenues for connection. As friends enter different life stages, understanding and respecting their new realities and constraints can help you adapt your expectations and interactions, ensuring the friendship continues thriving in its new context.

Navigating old and new friendships is a dynamic and ongoing process that enriches our lives in countless ways. By investing time and emotional energy into these relationships, you strengthen your support network and enjoy the irreplaceable joy that friendship brings. Whether reinforcing old ties or forging new ones, engaging with sincerity, empathy, and an open heart fosters connections that withstand time and change.

9.5 Handling Rejection and Disappointment in Relationships

Rejection and disappointment are as much a part of our relational landscapes as joy and connection. Yet, they sound a dark chord, often reverberating through our emotional foundations with unsettling intensity. Understanding these experiences' psychological impact is crucial for resilience and overall emotional health. Rejection from a friend, family member, or romantic partner can evoke a deep-seated fear of not being good enough, which taps into our fundamental need for belonging and acceptance. Disappointment, mainly when someone we trust lets us down, can shake the foundations of our trust, leading to feelings of betrayal and hurt. These emotions are natural responses to complex interpersonal dynamics, and acknowledging their validity is the first step in processing and overcoming them.

Coping with these feelings effectively requires a multifaceted approach. Self-reflection is a powerful tool, allowing you to explore your feelings deeply, understand the context of the rejection, and assess any personal growth opportunities that might emerge from the experience. This could involve journaling about your feelings, discussing the situation with a trusted friend, or seeking professional counseling to gain deeper insights. Additionally, leaning on your support system is vital. Friends, family, and church or community groups can offer comfort and perspectives that might help you see the situation in a new light. Focusing on personal growth is equally important; engage in activities that boost your self-esteem and help you reconnect with your intrinsic worth, such as pursuing a hobby, enhancing your skills, or contributing to your community. These activities reinforce your sense of self, independent of others' acceptance or approval.

Learning from rejection involves transforming painful experiences into opportunities for personal development and emotional strengthening. Each rejection provides unique insights into your values, expectations of others, and how you handle disappointment. By analyzing these situations, you can identify patterns contributing to recurring issues or discover areas of personal growth that need attention. For instance, if you're often upset by friends not meeting your expectations, you might need to communicate your needs more clearly or adjust what you expect from others. Adopting a mindset that views rejection as a path to greater self-awareness and resilience can dramatically change how you perceive and react to such experi-

ences, ultimately leading to more robust, more fulfilling relationships.

Maintaining self-esteem in the face of rejection is one of the most challenging yet essential aspects of our personal growth. It's easy to internalize rejection as a reflection of your worth, but it's necessary to distinguish between your value and the specific circumstances of the rejection. Practicing self-compassion is crucial; treat yourself with the same kindness and understanding you would offer a friend in a similar situation. Engage in positive self-talk that reinforces your strengths and worth, such as, "I am valued and loved regardless of this experience," or "I learn and grow from all life's challenges." These affirmations can help buffer the impact of rejection, safeguarding your self-esteem and preparing you for future relational challenges.

As this chapter closes, we recognize that navigating rejection and disappointment is integral to cultivating deeper personal relation-ships. Appropriate levels of engagement differ; only some relation-ships will deepen into friendship. Some friendships end; others begin. We live in an era of tremendous societal change. By under-standing the psychological impacts, embracing effective coping mechanisms, learning from each experience, and maintaining a robust sense of self-worth, we equip ourselves with the tools to survive and thrive despite these challenges. This preparation strengthens our current relationships and enriches our future inter-actions, making us more empathetic, resilient, and emotionally intel-ligent individuals. As we turn the page, we look forward to exploring further dimensions of personal relationships, continuing to build on the foundation of understanding and growth established here.

10

SPECIALIZED COMMUNICATION SCENARIOS

Imagine attending a bustling international conference, a melting pot of cultures, languages, and perspectives. Here, every handshake and greeting carries cultural nuances, and every conversation is a bridge between diverse worldviews. This scenario underscores the critical importance of cross-cultural competence in our increasingly globalized world, where effective communication across cultural boundaries is beneficial and imperative for success. Whether you're negotiating with overseas partners, collaborating with a multicultural team, or engaging with clients from different cultural backgrounds, understanding and navigating the complex landscape of cross-cultural communication is vital.

10.1 Cross-Cultural Communication: Techniques and Pitfalls

Cultural Competence

At the heart of successful cross-cultural communication lies cultural competence—the ability to interact effectively with people of different cultural and socio-economic backgrounds. Cultural competence involves more than just awareness of cultural differences; it requires understanding and respecting them, encompassing cultural norms, values, and etiquette. For example, while punctuality is highly valued in countries like Japan and Germany, more flexible attitudes towards time may be found in Latin America and the Middle East. Being culturally competent means you are prepared and adaptive to these differing values, which facilitates smoother interactions and helps build trust and respect. It entails a commitment to learning about other cultures continuously and applying this knowledge thoughtfully and respectfully in your interactions.

Common Cultural Pitfalls

Despite the best intentions, cross-cultural communication can sometimes lead to misunderstandings and misinterpretations due to common pitfalls. One significant challenge is the assumption of similarity, where one unconsciously expects people from different cultures to perceive, think, and react in the same way as they do. This assumption can lead to miscommunication and potential conflict. For instance, a direct communication style is standard in the U.S. and many Western cultures, where being transparent and straightforward is appreciated. However, in many Asian cultures, such an approach might be seen as aggressive or disrespectful; indirect communication is often preferred to maintain harmony and face. Another common pitfall includes misinterpreting non-verbal cues, such as gestures and body language, which can vary dramatically between cultures. As mentioned, the thumbs-up gesture is considered positive in many Western cultures but is offensive in parts of the Middle East and South America.

Techniques for Effective Cross-Cultural Communication

To navigate the complexities of cross-cultural communication effectively, several strategies can be employed:

• **Active Listening**: This involves listening for words and their meanings. It helps you understand what is being communicated and how different cultures perceive it. Attend closely to body language.

• **Clarification Questions**: When in doubt, asking questions can help clarify meanings and ensure all parties have the same understanding. This approach is essential in cross-cultural settings to avoid assumptions.

• **Use of Neutral, Universal Language:** It is crucial to avoid idioms, slang, and cultural references that may not translate well across cultures. Instead, using simple, clear, concise language can help prevent misunderstandings.

Case Studies of Cross-Cultural Success and Failures

To illustrate these points, consider the case of a U.S. marketing firm that collaborated with a Japanese company to launch a product. The American team used aggressive sales tactics and direct communication, which clashed with the Japanese team's approach of building relationships and trust first, leading to initial misunderstandings. However, the project eventually succeeded by implementing cross-cultural training for both teams, emphasizing the importance of understanding and respecting each other's communication styles. This led to a successful product launch in both countries.

In another instance, a multinational corporation faced challenges when it ignored cultural differences in advertising strategies across different regions. A successful ad campaign in Europe failed in Middle Eastern countries due to cultural misalignments in the messaging, which did not resonate with Middle Eastern cultural values and norms. This failure underscores the importance of cultural sensitivity and localization in global business strategies.

In conclusion, as you navigate your path in a world rich with cultural diversity, remember that the key to effective cross-cultural communication lies in understanding the broad strokes of cultural differences and appreciating the subtle nuances that define individual experiences. By cultivating a deep respect for these differences and continuously striving to improve your cultural competence, you can enhance your personal interactions and professional relationships across the globe.

10.2 Public Speaking: Engaging Your Audience Effectively

When stepping onto a stage, whether in front of a few colleagues or a vast auditorium, the essence of effective public speaking lies in your preparation and understanding of the audience. The importance of meticulously preparing cannot be overstated; it involves more than just rehearsing your lines. It starts with a deep dive into understanding who will be in your audience, their expectations, and what messages will likely resonate with them. For instance, addressing a group of seasoned industry professionals at a conference requires a different tone and level of detail than a workshop for novices. Researching your audience's demographic and psychographic characteristics provides insights that help tailor your speech to meet their interests and needs, ensuring relevance that captivates and engages.

Moreover, the structure of your speech plays a pivotal role in retaining the audience's attention. Begin with a clear, engaging introduction that outlines what your audience can expect to gain from listening to you. This could be an intriguing question, a surprising statistic, or a compelling story, setting the tone for the rest of your presentation. As you transition into the main body, keep your content organized into distinct segments, each with a clear message supported by examples, data, or anecdotes. This clarity keeps the audience engaged, as they can easily follow your train of thought without becoming overwhelmed by too much information at once. Finally, conclude firmly by summarizing the key points and, if appropriate, providing a call to action. This could be an invitation to adopt a new business strategy, a recommendation to support a cause, or a directive to implement new knowledge in daily practices.

Engagement goes beyond words; it's about connecting with the audience throughout your presentation. Techniques such as storytelling can transform your speech from a monologue into an immersive experience. You make your content more relatable and memorable by weaving critical points into a narrative. Rhetorical questions are another powerful tool, provoking thought and encouraging listeners to reflect on how the information relates to their situations. When used appropriately, humor can lighten the mood and help build a rapport with your audience, making your speech more enjoyable and engaging. Additionally, incorporating interactive elements like Q&A sessions not only breaks the monotony but also gives the audience a chance to clarify doubts and engage directly with you, enhancing the overall impact of your presentation.

Managing public speaking anxiety is a common challenge, yet it's a hurdle you can overcome with strategic approaches. One effective technique is focused breathing, which can help calm your nerves and reduce anxiety before and during your speech. Practice deep, slow breathing exercises to steady your heartbeat and clear your mind, preparing you mentally to face the audience. Regular practice of your speech is also crucial; familiarity with your content can significantly boost your confidence, making it easier to deliver your speech fluently, even when nerves kick in. During practice sessions, simulate the speaking environment as closely as possible, including practicing with the technology you will use, such as microphones or slide changers.

Additionally, focus on the message you want to convey rather than on yourself. Shifting your mindset from your performance to your message's importance can alleviate pressure and elevate your delivery. Remember, your primary goal is to communicate a message effectively, not to deliver a flawless performance. Embracing this perspective can transform your public speaking experiences, turning them from sources of anxiety into opportunities for impactful communication.

10.3 Crisis Communication: Keeping Calm and Effective Under Pressure

Navigating the unpredictable waters of a crisis requires a robust strategy and a cool head. Effective crisis communication is pivotal in managing the immediate repercussions and shaping long-term perceptions and trust. Clarity, accuracy, and promptness are the cornerstones of sound crisis communication. Each message must be crystal clear to prevent misunderstandings further complicating the situation. Accuracy is non-negotiable, as providing reliable, fact-checked information builds credibility and trust. Promptness in communication ensures that you control the narrative, preventing misinformation and speculation from filling the void.

Preparing for potential crises involves more than just a theoretical plan; it requires a practical, actionable strategy that is understood and embraced by all levels of an organization. This preparation includes defining clear roles for who will speak on behalf of the organization, determining the channels through which communications will be disseminated, and crafting key messages that address potential scenarios. This proactive approach enhances the organization's ability to respond swiftly and effectively and instills confidence among stakeholders, reassuring them that the organization is well-equipped to handle challenges. For instance, a company might conduct regular training sessions for its crisis communication team, ensuring everyone knows their roles and responsibilities and can respond quickly. Additionally, simulations or drills can be used to test the robustness of the communication plan, allowing for adjustments before a real crisis strikes.

Communicating under pressure is a skill that can be honed with practice and mindfulness. When a crisis unfolds, the instinct may be to react swiftly, which can lead to rushed or emotional responses. Instead, focusing on the facts helps maintain a grounded perspective, essential for clear communication. Transparency is crucial; openly sharing what is known and what is not known and the steps to manage the situation can help maintain public trust. Managing the emotional tone of communications is also vital. It's about striking the right balance between showing empathy and maintaining a professional demeanor. Techniques such as pausing before responding to gather thoughts or using calming breaths can help maintain composure, ensuring that communications are not only effective but also measured and considerate.

Post-crisis communication is critical in rebuilding and maintaining trust. It involves continuing the transparency demonstrated during the crisis and sharing what has been learned and what measures have been put in place to prevent future crises. This phase is about reflection and growth, showing stakeholders that the organization is committed to continual improvement. Communicating post-crisis also involves acknowledging mistakes and outlining how they will be addressed. This openness humanizes the organization and demonstrates a commitment to ethical standards and accountability.

In wrapping up this exploration into the dynamics of crisis communication, remember that the principles of clarity, accuracy, and promptness are your guiding stars. You can confidently communicate during crises by preparing comprehensively, maintaining composure under pressure, and embracing transparency. These strategies are about managing crises and turning challenges into opportunities for strengthening trust and credibility. As we close this chapter, let's carry forward these insights, ready to face challenges head-on, knowing that effective communication is critical to surviving and thriving in adversity.

EPILOGUE

As we reach the end of our journey through the intricate communication landscape, let's take a moment to reflect on the ground we've covered. From the basics of crafting engaging introductions and understanding the psychology of first impressions to mastering the art of listening and navigating the complex digital communication landscape, we've explored a comprehensive array of strategies that empower both introverts and extroverts alike. We explored emotional intelligence, an essential skill in enhancing our interactions, and tackled the challenges of various specialized communication scenarios, each adding depth to our toolkit.

Communication, as you've seen, is a universal human challenge. It transcends personality types, professional environments, and personal situations. Each chapter of this book was structured to ensure that no matter where you stand on the spectrum of introversion or extroversion, there are adaptable strategies to be implemented in your unique circumstances. Whether improving your digital rapport or enhancing face-to-face interactions, the aim was always precise: to make you a more effective communicator.

The power of effective communication cannot be overstated. As illustrated throughout our discussions, sharpening your communication skills can dramatically deepen personal relationships and accelerate professional success. Imagine the doors that could open if every conversation you engaged in was approached with confidence and awareness. Many individuals have changed their life's trajectory simply by harnessing the principles of transparent and empathetic dialogue. This is the empowerment that effective communication brings, making you capable of shaping your path.

As you step forward, I urge you to keep the key takeaways from each chapter close to your heart. Regular self-reflection is crucial. Know thyself. Assess your communication strengths and areas for improvement. Set realistic, achievable goals using the strategies we've explored. Begin by enhancing your listening skills or crafting more impactful digital communications, and gradually expand your efforts as you grow more confident and skilled.

Please view this book as something other than a checklist to be completed but as a companion on a lifelong journey. Becoming an exceptional communicator is never-ending—no final destination exists. Each conversation offers a new opportunity to apply a technique, reflect on its effectiveness, and refine your approach. The world around us is ever-changing, always presenting new challenges. This ongoing journey keeps us motivated and committed to our growth as communicators.

Share your progress and challenges with me. Connect on LinkedIn. Your stories of transformation and everyday victories in communication inspire me to continue researching and sharing this vital skill. Your contributions are invaluable, and they make our community vibrant. Let's build a community where growth is celebrated, and knowledge is shared freely.

Finally, remember that the ability to communicate effectively is within your reach. It does not require perfection. Let this be your inspiration: every word you speak, every message you send, is a step towards becoming a more empowered, effective communicator.

Thank you for joining me on this journey. Here's to speaking and listening effectively and meaningfully. Let's continue learning from each other, and may your communications be fruitful and fulfilling!

A LAST REQUEST

If you believe others might benefit from reading this book, please leave a review on Amazon. It would also help me to produce more books, as "the algorithm" rules on Amazon.

If you are reading this on an ebook please click here to be taken to the review page.

If you are reading a print book, please scan the QR code below to access the review page.

Thank you!

BIBLIOGRAPHY

4 Tips To Stop Negative Thoughts With NLP. Retrieved from https://goodthingsaregonnacome.com/4-tips-to-stop-negative-thoughts-with-nlp/

Summary: This practical guide offers four NLP-based strategies for overcoming negative thoughts, aiming to improve mental well-being and foster a more positive mindset.

10 Ways NLP Enhances Leadership. Retrieved from https://www.linkedin.com/pulse/10-ways-nlp-enhances-leadership-sarah-merron

Summary: This article discusses ten ways in which NLP can improve leadership skills, emphasizing techniques for effective communication, influence, and personal development.

Case studies - The Association for Neuro Linguistic... Retrieved from https://anlp.org/case-studies

Summary: This collection of case studies demonstrates the practical applications of NLP in various settings, showcasing its effectiveness in addressing different personal and professional challenges.

Creating Smarter Online Communities with NLP and Network... Retrieved from https://adibarua2002.medium.com/creating-smarter-online-communities-with-nlp-and-network-analytics-147810d3cee5

Summary: This article explores the use of NLP and network analytics in building smarter online communities, focusing on enhancing communication, engagement, and collaboration.

Effectiveness of NLP in Dealing with Guilt Induced Anxiety... Retrieved from https://ijip.in/articles/effectiveness-of-nlp-in-dealing-with-guilt-induced-anxiety-depression-and-stress-a-case-study/

Summary: This case study examines the effectiveness of NLP interventions in addressing guilt-induced anxiety, depression, and stress, highlighting positive therapeutic outcomes.

EFFECTIVENESS OF NEURO-LINGUISTIC... Retrieved from https://www.afjbs.com/uploads/paper/2a097edbbf07f9fa4fe7850f51c87781.pdf

Summary: This paper evaluates the effectiveness of NLP interventions in various contexts, presenting evidence from multiple studies to support its use in enhancing personal and professional outcomes.

Evidence-based Neuro Linguistic Psychotherapy: a meta-... Retrieved from https://pubmed.ncbi.nlm.nih.gov/26609647/

Summary: This meta-analysis evaluates the effectiveness of neuro-linguistic psychotherapy, summarizing the evidence from various studies to determine its impact on mental health outcomes.

FAQ: What Are Self-Assessment Tools? (Plus Examples). Retrieved from https://www. indeed.com/career-advice/career-development/self-assessment-tools
Summary: This FAQ page provides an overview of self-assessment tools, including examples and explanations of how they can be used for personal and professional development.

Five trends in NLP and NLG for 2023 | Narrativa. Retrieved from https://www.narra tiva.com/5-trends-in-nlp-and-nlg-for-2023/
Summary: This article identifies and explores five emerging trends in NLP and Natural Language Generation (NLG) for 2023, discussing their potential impact and applications.

History of NLP. Retrieved from https://nlpea.com/international-nlp-association-of-excellence-nlpea/history-nlp
Summary: This article outlines the historical development of NLP, tracing its origins, key figures, and the evolution of its methodologies over time.

How Active Listening Can Improve Conflict Resolution. Retrieved from https://www. opteamize.io/articles/article/The%20Art%20of%20Listening
Summary: This article highlights the importance of active listening in conflict resolution, discussing how NLP techniques can enhance listening skills and resolve conflicts effectively.

How To Control Your Emotions Using NLP - Premier Life Coach. Retrieved from https://www.westchesterpalifecoach.com/post/how-to-control-your-emotions-using-nlp
Summary: This article offers insights into using NLP techniques to control and manage emotions, promoting emotional intelligence and well-being.

How To Use NLP Techniques To Increase Your Productivity? Retrieved from https:// www.iienstitu.com/en/blog/how-to-use-nlp-techniques-to-increase-your-produc tivity
Summary: This article discusses how NLP techniques can be employed to boost productivity, offering practical tips for integrating NLP strategies into daily routines.

Management of Panic Attacks through Timeline Therapy... Retrieved from https:// pjmr.org.pk/index.php/pjmr/article/view/93
Summary: This study investigates the use of NLP's Timeline Therapy in managing panic attacks, presenting evidence of its effectiveness in reducing symptoms and improving mental health.

Mastering Milton: Erickson's Hypnotic Language Patterns. Retrieved from https:// www.jacquinhypnosisacademy.com/blog/miltonerickson
Summary: This resource delves into the hypnotic language patterns developed by Milton Erickson, explaining their application within NLP for therapeutic and influential purposes.

Mental training for young athlete: A case of study of NLP... Retrieved from https:// www.sciencedirect.com/science/article/pii/S2666560322000160
Summary: This case study examines the use of NLP techniques in mental training for

young athletes, highlighting its benefits in enhancing performance and psychological resilience.

Meta Programs and the power of influence. Retrieved from https://www.tonyrobbins.com/stories/leadership-academy/influential-power-meta-programs/

Summary: This article explains meta programs in NLP, which are patterns of thinking that influence behavior and decision-making, and how they can be used to enhance influence and leadership.

Neuro–Linguistic Programming (NLP) Principles and... Retrieved from https://www.businessballs.com/emotional-intelligence/neuro-linguistic-programming/

Summary: This resource provides an overview of the principles and techniques of NLP, explaining how they can be applied to improve emotional intelligence and communication skills.

NLP and Neuroplasticity - Info by Matt Cole. Retrieved from https://tinyurl.com/53b6s7ut

Summary: This article explores the relationship between NLP and neuroplasticity, discussing how NLP techniques can facilitate the creation of new neural connections and promote mental flexibility.

NLP for Stress Management. Retrieved from https://internalchange.com/nlp-stress-management/

Summary: This guide explores various NLP strategies for managing stress, providing practical tools for reducing anxiety and improving overall mental health.

NLP swish technique for changing behaviors. Retrieved from https://nlpsure.com/nlp-swish-technique-for-changing-behaviors/

Summary: This article introduces the NLP swish technique, a method for altering unwanted behaviors and thought patterns by creating new mental associations.

NLP Techniques for Effective Communication. Retrieved from https://themindpower.in/blog/nlp-techniques-for-effective-communication/

Summary: This resource outlines NLP techniques aimed at improving communication skills, facilitating better understanding, and more impactful interactions.

Setting SMART Goals Using NLP: A Path to Success. Retrieved from https://nlp4lifemastery.com/2024/02/10/setting-smart-goals-using-nlp-a-path-to-success/

Summary: This article outlines how to set SMART (Specific, Measurable, Achievable, Relevant, Time-bound) goals using NLP techniques, aiming to enhance goal-setting and achievement processes.

The Milton-Model: The Language of Influence and Being... Retrieved from https://spencerinstitute.com/the-milton-model-nlp/

Summary: This resource explains the Milton-Model, a set of NLP language patterns designed to influence and guide communication, named after the renowned hypnotherapist Milton Erickson.

Use this NLP Morning Ritual to kick start your day towards... Retrieved from https://www.abbyeagle.com/nlp-coaching-resources/start-the-day-right.php

Summary: This guide offers a morning ritual based on NLP techniques to start the day positively and productively, enhancing mental and emotional readiness for daily challenges.

Ethical challenges of neuro-linguistic programming. Retrieved from https://www.tandfonline.com/doi/abs/10.1080/24721735.2022.2101741

Summary: This paper discusses the ethical considerations and challenges associated with the use of NLP, emphasizing the importance of ethical practices in applying NLP techniques.

Ackerman, C. E. (2021, July 12). Conflict resolution in relationships & couples: 5 strategies. PositivePsychology.com. Retrieved from https://positivepsychology.com/conflict-resolution-relationships/

Summary: This article provides five strategies for resolving conflicts in relationships and couples, emphasizing the importance of effective communication and emotional understanding.

AdvisoryCloud. (n.d.). How to improve your active listening skills as a VP of sustainability. AdvisoryCloud. Retrieved from https://advisorycloud.com/blog/how-to-improve-your-active-listening-skills-as-a-vp-of-sustainability

Summary: This guide offers tips for improving active listening skills, specifically tailored for VPs of sustainability, highlighting techniques to enhance communication and leadership.

An elevator pitch is a brief persuasive speech that you use. Retrieved from https://helpinhomework.org/question/35266/An-elevator-pitch-is-a-brief-persuasive-speech-that-you-use-to-spark-interest-in-a-project-idea-o

Summary: This article explains the concept of an elevator pitch and provides guidelines for crafting an effective pitch to spark interest in a project or idea.

Army and Navy Academy. (2021, April 7). Effective communication is critical to resolving conflicts. Army and Navy Academy. Retrieved from https://www.armyandnavyacademy.org/blog/effective-communication-is-key-to-resolving-conflicts/

Summary: This blog post discusses the importance of effective communication in resolving conflicts, offering practical tips for improving communication skills.

Axero Solutions. (2021, July 20). How to communicate with your boss at work - 10 tips to improve corporate communications. Axero Solutions Blog. Retrieved from https://axerosolutions.com/blog/how-to-communicate-with-your-boss-at-work-10-tips-to-improve-corporate-communications

Summary: This article provides ten tips for communicating effectively with your boss, aimed at improving corporate communications and building better professional relationships.

BetterUp Editorial Team. (2021, October 19). How to read body language and gain deeper emotional understanding. BetterUp. Retrieved from https://www.betterup.com/blog/how-to-read-body-language

Summary: This guide explores the importance of reading body language in gaining deeper emotional understanding, offering practical tips for improving nonverbal communication skills.

Business.com Editorial Team. (2021, September 14). Should you use emojis in business communications? Business.com. Retrieved from https://www.business.com/articles/put-an-emoji-on-it-should-you-use-emojis-in-business-communication/

Summary: This article discusses the pros and cons of using emojis in business communications, providing guidelines for their appropriate use in professional settings.

Calm Editorial Team. (2021, September 8). Mindful listening: How to improve your communication. Calm Blog. Retrieved from https://www.calm.com/blog/mindful-listening

Summary: This blog post offers tips for practicing mindful listening, aimed at improving communication skills and fostering better interpersonal relationships.

Castrillon, C. (2021, January 21). How to craft a knockout elevator pitch. Forbes. Retrieved from https://www.forbes.com/sites/carolinecastrillon/2021/01/21/how-to-craft-a-knockout-elevator-pitch/

Summary: This article provides a step-by-step guide for crafting an effective elevator pitch, aimed at capturing the attention of potential clients or investors.

Cherry, K. (2021, July 7). Understanding the dimensions of introversion & shyness. Verywell Mind. Retrieved from https://www.verywellmind.com/introversion-and-shyness-explained-3024882

Summary: This article explains the differences between introversion and shyness, providing insights into their dimensions and how they affect behavior and social interactions.

Cherry, K. (2022, September 30). 7 active listening techniques for better communication. Verywell Mind. Retrieved from https://www.verywellmind.com/what-is-active-listening-3024343

Summary: This guide offers seven techniques for practicing active listening, aimed at improving communication skills and enhancing personal and professional relationships.

Cialdini, R. B. (n.d.). Dr. Robert Cialdini's seven principles of persuasion. Influence at Work. Retrieved from https://www.influenceatwork.com/7-principles-of-persuasion/

Summary: This article outlines Dr. Robert Cialdini's seven principles of persuasion, providing insights into how they can be applied to influence others effectively.

Decker, B. (2016, August 23). 6 steps for effectively connecting with your audience. Decker Communications. Retrieved from https://www.yourthoughtpartner.com/blog/6-steps-for-effectively-connecting-with-your-audiences

Summary: This article provides six steps for effectively connecting with your audience during presentations, aimed at enhancing engagement and communication impact.

Development Dimensions International (DDI). (2022, May 23). Using emotional intelligence to improve communication. DDI World. Retrieved from https://www.ddiworld.com/blog/emotional-intelligence-and-communication

Summary: This blog post explores the role of emotional intelligence in improving communication, offering strategies for developing emotional awareness and effective interaction skills.

Forbes Editorial Team. (2021, May 25). 10 strategies and techniques for speaking engagement success. LinkedIn Pulse. Retrieved from https://www.linkedin.com/pulse/10-strategies-techniques-speaking-engagement-success-laura-katen

Summary: This article provides ten strategies and techniques for achieving success in speaking engagements, emphasizing preparation, delivery, and audience connection.

Forbes Editorial Team. (2023, October 3). **5 strategies for cross-cultural communication across global teams.** Forbes. Retrieved from https://www.forbes.com/sites/rachelwells/2023/10/03/5-strategies-for-cross-cultural-communication-across-global-teams/

Summary: This article discusses five strategies for effective cross-cultural communication within global teams, highlighting the importance of cultural awareness and adaptability.

Goman, C. K. (2011, May 31). **The art and science of mirroring.** Forbes. Retrieved from https://www.forbes.com/sites/carolkinseygoman/2011/05/31/the-art-and-science-of-mirroring/

Summary: This article explores the technique of mirroring in communication, discussing its psychological basis and practical applications for building rapport and influence.

HubSpot. (2022, February 15). **Email etiquette: 27 rules to make a perfect impression on your readers.** HubSpot Blog. Retrieved from https://blog.hubspot.com/sales/email-etiquette-tips-rules

Summary: This guide offers 27 rules for practicing good email etiquette, aimed at making a positive impression on readers and enhancing professional communication.

Indeed Editorial Team. (2021, October 19). **8 effective networking strategies for professionals.** Indeed Career Guide. Retrieved from https://www.indeed.com/career-advice/career-development/networking-strategies

Summary: This article provides eight strategies for effective networking, aimed at helping professionals build meaningful connections and advance their careers.

Indeed Editorial Team. (2022, May 16). **Importance of first impressions (And how to improve yours). Indeed Career Guide.** Retrieved from https://uk.indeed.com/career-advice/career-development/importance-of-first-impressions

Summary: This article discusses the importance of first impressions and offers tips for improving how you present yourself in professional settings.

LinkedIn Career Expert. (2021, June 3). **How to build an online presence for career growth. LinkedIn.** Retrieved from https://www.linkedin.com/advice/0/how-can-you-build-effective-online-presence-ovnje

Summary: This guide offers advice on building an effective online presence for career growth, emphasizing the importance of networking and personal branding.

Manes, S., & Manes, R. (2021, September 14). **Communication: The heart of a relationship. Postgraduate Medical Journal, 93(1105), 570-573.**

Summary: This article explores the central role of communication in relationships, discussing various strategies for improving communication and fostering stronger connections.

Mayo Clinic Staff. (2021, March 25). **Fear of public speaking: How can I overcome it?** Mayo Clinic. Retrieved from https://www.mayoclinic.org/diseases-conditions/

specific-phobias/expert-answers/fear-of-public-speaking/faq-20058416

Summary: This article offers tips for overcoming the fear of public speaking, providing practical advice for managing anxiety and improving presentation skills.

Mind Tools Content Team. (2021, August 16). **Improving group dynamics - Helping your team work more effectively. Mind Tools.** Retrieved from https://www.mindtools.com/ad3z8yv/improving-group-dynamics

Summary: This article explores strategies for improving group dynamics, aimed at helping teams work more effectively and cohesively.

Mind Tools Content Team. (2022, January 10). **How to follow up after networking - Turn new contacts into lasting connections. Mind Tools.** Retrieved from https://www.mindtools.com/a8pjz5d/how-to-follow-up-after-networking

Summary: This guide offers tips for following up after networking events, aimed at turning new contacts into lasting professional relationships.

National Institute of Mental Health (NIMH). (2021, June). **Social anxiety disorder: More than just shyness. NIMH Health Information.** Retrieved from https://www.nimh.nih.gov/health/publications/social-anxiety-disorder-more-than-just-shyness

Summary: This article provides an overview of social anxiety disorder, discussing its symptoms, causes, and treatment options.

Practical Intimacy Team. (2021, May 5). **9 powerful intimacy exercises to feel more connected. Practical Intimacy.** Retrieved from https://practicalintimacy.com/marriage-intimacy-exercises-for-couples/

Summary: This article offers nine intimacy exercises designed to help couples feel more connected and enhance their relationship.

Roberge, K. (2021, November 1). **How to have more meaningful conversations. Psyche.** Retrieved from https://psyche.co/guides/how-to-have-more-meaningful-conversations

Summary: This guide provides tips for having more meaningful conversations, aimed at deepening connections and improving communication skills.

Robert Half. (2021, December 7). **14 videoconference etiquette tips. Robert Half.** Retrieved from https://www.roberthalf.com/us/en/insights/career-development/14-video-conference-etiquette-tips

Summary: This article offers 14 tips for practicing good videoconference etiquette, aimed at improving professional communication in virtual meetings.

Sender, D. (2017, October 4). **How to give and receive feedback effectively. Postgraduate Medical Journal,** 93(1105), 570-573.

Summary: This article discusses strategies for giving and receiving feedback effectively, aimed at fostering better communication and personal development.

Shortform Editorial Team. (n.d.). **How to use body language to make a good first impression. Shortform.** Retrieved from https://www.shortform.com/blog/body-language-first-impression/#:~=Do%20nonverbal%20cues%20play%20a

Summary: This guide discusses the importance of body language in making a good first impression, offering tips for using nonverbal cues effectively.

Stanford Graduate School of Business. (2021, June 21). **Make 'em laugh: How humor can be the secret weapon in your communication. Stanford Graduate School of**

Business. Retrieved from https://www.gsb.stanford.edu/insights/make-em-laugh-how-humor-can-be-secret-weapon-your-communication

Summary: This article explores the role of humor in communication, discussing how it can be used as a tool to engage and influence others.

Thaler, R. (2020). **Enhancing human rights through AI applications. AI and Ethics,** 1(1), 15-24.

Summary: This paper discusses the potential of AI applications to enhance human rights, exploring ethical considerations and practical implementations.

Weir, K. (2012, May 1). **The psychological study of smiling. Observer.** Retrieved from https://www.psychologicalscience.org/observer/the-psychological-study-of-smiling

Summary: This article explores the psychological aspects of smiling, discussing its effects on social interactions and emotional well-being.

Weir, K. (2023, November). **Conversations are essential to our well-being. Psychologists explain why. American Psychological Association.** Retrieved from https://www.apa.org/monitor/2023/11/conversations-key-to-wellbeing#:~=Pre%2D%20and%20post%2Dsurveys%20indicated

Summary: This article discusses the importance of conversations for mental and emotional well-being, providing insights from psychologists on the benefits of meaningful communication.

Wells, R. (2023, October 3). **5 strategies for cross-cultural communication across global teams. Forbes.** Retrieved from https://www.forbes.com/sites/rachelwells/2023/10/03/5-strategies-for-cross-cultural-communication-across-global-teams/

Summary: This article discusses five strategies for effective cross-cultural communication within global teams, highlighting the importance of cultural awareness and adaptability.

Wharton Executive Education. (2021, May 1). **Influencing without authority: A four-part formula. Wharton at Work.** Retrieved from https://executiveeducation.wharton.upenn.edu/thought-leadership/wharton-at-work/2021/05/influencing-without-authority/

Summary: This article provides a four-part formula for influencing others without authority, aimed at enhancing leadership and communication skills.

Yoh Services LLC. (2020, July 2). **Always be learning: 5 strategies for lifelong learners. Yoh Blog.** Retrieved from https://www.yoh.com/blog/5-strategies-for-lifelong-learners

Summary: This article offers five strategies for lifelong learning, emphasizing the importance of continuous education and personal growth.

ABOUT THE AUTHOR

Elliott Middleton PhD lives with his family in the Nashville, Tennessee, area.